– Updated and revised edition –

PATINA
VOLKSWAGENS

Mark Walker

T0405901

Also from Veloce

www.veloce.co.uk

First published hardback in February 2019, reprinted in paperback in December 2022 by Veloce Publishing Limited, Veloce House, Parkway Farm Business Park, Middle Farm Way, Poundbury, Dorchester DT1 3AR, England.
Tel +44 (0)1305 260068 / Fax 01305 250479 / e-mail info@veloce.co.uk / web www.veloce.co.uk or www.velocebooks.com.
ISBN: 978-1-787119-27-7; UPC: 6-36847-01927-3.

– Updated and revised edition –

PATINA
VOLKSWAGENS

Mark Walker

VELOCE PUBLISHING
THE PUBLISHER OF FINE AUTOMOTIVE BOOKS

Contents

Cover image: courtesy Fabien Becasse. Endpapers: courtesy Shin Watanabe.

Acknowledgements

It's so hard to write acknowledgements, for fear of missing someone out. Firstly, I'd like to thank everyone (too many to name individually) who took the time to contribute pictures of their cars, from arranging photo shoots to digging out photos from their archives, purely for their love of Patina Volkswagens. Car owners, wherever possible, have been credited in the captions, as have the picture owners.

Apologies must go to the people whose cars haven't made it into the book; despite the inauspicious start, when I realised that most of the photos I'd taken over the last 15 years were too low resolution for the publisher, I was overwhelmed with offers of incredible cars, and have weaved as many as possible into the book. Choosing 300 plus images from the thousands I received was, literally, agonising.

To the Colin Burnhams and Keith Seumes of this world, the guys who put VW books together before the digital age, and who I've always looked up to, I doff my hat; I can't imagine how painstaking it would have been putting a book like this together without social media and digital image transmission. I'm hugely grateful to both for their input and support of this book.

I really couldn't have put *Patina Volkswagens* together without the many awesome people that make the VW scene such a great community to be a part of; this book is for you.

I'd like to thank my parents for always supporting my car hobby, from giving me pocket money to buy magazines to taking me to shows and abiding my never-ending car talk (even though no one else in my family was into cars). I'd like to thank my mum, especially, for helping me to buy, and fix up, my first Beetle at age 16. Also, my great uncle Lawrence Greenwell (RIP) for patiently showing me how to deal with the challenges of working on old cars; he was always just a phone call away and would often spontaneously pop round, after my SOS call, to help in person.

Big thanks to Robin Russell-Pavier, a former Beetle owner, who had boundless words of encouragement and enthusiasm for the book, and was an expert proofreader.

Lastly, but by no means least, I owe a huge debt of gratitude to my better half, Joanna (Jojo) Cooke, for not only encouraging me to finish my book proposal and find a publisher, but also for being so supportive during the whole process: from her brilliant proofreading, professional marketing and social media advice, to empowering me to carry on when I hit one of the many stumbling blocks.

The author picking up a new project in 2016: an original paint L456 Ruby Red Beetle from Sweden, with plenty of Patina.

About the author

Mark Walker bought his first 1964 VW Beetle at age 16, before he could legally drive. Over 25 years of VW ownership and more than 100 air-cooled Volkswagens have now passed by since that point. Mark was the owner and operator of The Bus Station (2002-2013) and Vintage Werks (2006-2007), companies heavily immersed in the VW scene and known for importing classic Volkswagens from around the world, carrying out sympathetic restoration work, and gaining an international reputation for out of the box thinking, high-quality suspension modifications and turning out magazine feature-worthy cars. The success and popularity of his business earned him the nickname 'Slam King.' Mark has written for *VolksWorld* and *Camper & Bus* magazines since 2012.

Introduction

When are you going to paint it?

My love of old cars, especially Volkswagens, started at a young age – 12 years old – when I began buying car magazines. In the UK, at that time, *Street Machine* and *Custom Car* were really the only choices if you were into old, cool, modified cars, especially VWs. That is until the launch of *VolksWorld* in 1987.

In the last 32 years I've bought every book and magazine that I could, with some of my own cars even featured in the later years; in 2012, it was a dream come true when I started writing first for *VolksWorld Camper & Bus* and then *VolksWorld,* and I'm proud to still be regularly writing for them today.

Since my first Beetle, a 1964 model, at the age of 16, I have gone on to own over 100 air-cooled VWs. I've traversed the globe to rummage through junkyards, meet dealers and collectors, and visit many of the world's best VW shows.

In all the time that I've owned old Volkswagens, I've never owned a fully restored one, as I have always favoured nice original cars over newly painted or restored ones.

For myself, and many others, the obsession with owning original paint cars has taken over. Why original paint? There are several reasons, but in the main, it's because original paint cars aren't hiding anything, and have much more character than restored ones. At VW shows I often find myself walking by a lot of restored cars – as pretty as they are, any interesting semblances of history have somehow been eclipsed once the new paint went on. Another key reason is uniqueness – it's pretty hard to just go out and create an original car. Stone chips, paint that has been burned-off by the sun, and genuine Patina markings are one of a kind, their unique look so attractive to the eye.

Bob Van Heyst (owner of BBT in Belgium and curator of his own Volkswagen museum) couldn't have put it more perfectly: "You can paint a lot of fun out of a car." Owners of shiny restored cars tend to develop a fear of using them, and the cars all too often end up locked away for safekeeping, taking the enjoyment out of the hobby.

Patina cars, on the other hand, give you the freedom to use them as intended and admire them as cars with character, and rich, visible histories. Even as a child I could never understand why people kept their toy cars in the original boxes, in mint condition – all of mine were well worn, battered, and bruised, and my full-sized cars today are no exception; they are more interesting with Patina.

It's not just VW owners that think original paint is cool either. Patina has long been a buzzword in the antiques world, and a couple of the more famous on-screen treasure hunters even own classic Patina VWs (see Chapter Five). The increase in popularity of salvage and restoration themed TV shows has certainly helped to bring Patina and Patina cars to the fore; who would have thought, even five years ago, that Patina cars would be getting such mainstream interest across the globe.

What I love most about this cultural shift is that it demonstrates, to the masses, that owning an unrestored car is not for lazy or penniless people, but a choice to preserve something, rather than eradicating any character or historical significance by setting the odometer back to zero as part of making it look new again.

Now, more than ever, people are beginning to appreciate Patina and embrace it; stop to fill up a Patina car with fuel and, whereas once upon a time people would be asking when you're going to paint it, nowadays there seems to be more appreciation of how cool it looks. That said, it's not the approval of others that drives many of the people whose cars you'll see in this book. For them, like me, it's a true gratefulness for the character of old things; be it cars, antiques or memorabilia – who cares if other people like it, we do! The age-old phrase "One man's junk is another man's treasure" comes to mind; some of us love what other people see as scrap, and this book proves, beyond all doubt, that Patina today is a conscious choice and deserves to be embraced by the world.

The idea for this book first came to me in 2013 when I realised the growing interest in original paint Patina cars. They were being featured more and more in VW magazines but there weren't any books on the subject. *Patina Volkswagens* is the first book of its kind and I am honoured to be able to share my love, understanding, and appreciation with you, a fellow Patina lover. This book recognises the Patina movement from its humble, misunderstood beginnings to its now iconic status, and captures a moment in time that can be treasured forever.

Many of us long-time Patina car owners predicted that, one day, the monetary value of these cars would start to exceed that of restored cars, and we have been proved right; never has this been truer than when comedian Jerry Seinfeld famously came out as the highest bidder on an original paint 1958 Porsche Speedster. The auction price of $583,000 proves that more than one person that day valued a car with genuine, untouched Patina. Jerry, a long-time classic VW and Porsche enthusiast, has allowed us to publish a picture of that car, and some direct quotes from him, later in the book (see Chapter Five).

Although the rising prices may put some cars financially out of reach for many of us who've cherished them all our lives, at least the cars are being valued and preserved for decades to come; this alone means that the Patina won't be lost forever in a restoration.

Let's not eradicate all traces of history when it comes to cars. Don't lock them away for fear of clocking up too many miles. Love their imperfections, enjoy them as they are, and, most importantly, get them out on the road – it's what cars were meant for.

The author driving his old original paint 1963 Mouse Grey Bus in 2013.

Foreword

By Drew Pritchard

Drew Pritchard (left), pictured with the author.

Patina is an overused word, misunderstood by most; looking at the *Oxford English Dictionary* definition doesn't really help much either. For me, having some Patina in most things I own or buy is everything. It may be considered 'rust' by the uninformed. Many will think it needs to be painted or restored. To those who are even more uninformed, it's a fake, rattle can job, something that can be created by sanding off paint and allowing things to rust. To the people that get Patina – *real* Patina – it's a rare beast that only improves with time.

Patina can be faked and faked well, but it'll still be a lie. It's a buzzword at the moment, but will fade again, left for those of us in the know to enjoy. Patina adds value, but those of us who understand it don't care, and rightly so.

Patina, to me, is love for a car that you use every day, as a tool to get to work, to do the school run, to go to the shops. It's a car that was kept and used as it was intended to be, but never abused – 50 years of turning the key, 40 years of opening the engine lid to check the oil, 30 years of rain all week and being washed on a Sunday, dried off with a chamois leather and put away.

Patina can be a scratch, a dent, a period repair – bad or good – but it's honest, and a part of the car's history; I'll never paint my car if it gets scratched. Even if I need to change a panel for some reason, I'll leave it unmatched (I just scratched the wing on my '52 Beetle but it's there now, and that's where it'll stay). To repair is now the norm, ingrained in us by insurance companies and social constraints.

In the past, you bought a car to use and keep, not to change every three years; you lived with it and cared for it (or not). When it stopped working it was repaired and used again, until it broke and was fixed again. My own car, featured in this book, is a case in point; it was bought new in Ireland as an indirect import from a farmer who had a shed and a side line. The first owner kept it for a long time and used it every day – it was his favourite. When the engine gave up it was pushed into the barn for safe keeping, another Bug was bought, and the cycle continued. I then became the next owner; I bought the car because it told me a story, and, as silly as it may sound to some people, it spoke to me. I understood it, and I would fix it just enough to be usable again and then leave it alone, continuing the story … this is my 'keeper' Beetle – there won't be another, shinier replacement.

The dashboard in my car is a particular joy, nothing that I can see has ever been removed, altered or replaced since the day it left Wolfsburg; the key is worn to ten per cent of what it was, the ash tray is seized closed, the switches have yellowed, but it's original and *that* is the point.

"Patina is wear that has happened to the original." My life with antiques and VWs has always been just so; it's a long story, but I'm sure those reading this book already understand.

Patina is life; we and our cars wear it. Enjoy.

CHAPTER ONE

From shaky foundations

A cult car is born

What hasn't been written about the VW Beetle, Bus, and all other air-cooled derivatives could, I'm sure, be contained on the back of a postage stamp. Never has one automotive brand captured our imagination so much, or for so long. Hundreds of books about these cars have been printed over the past 50 years, which give a detailed rundown of the foundation of the Volkswagen: conceived by Ferdinand Porsche, funded by Hitler, and resurrected from the ashes of war by British service personnel. Let's start by saying that telling that particular story in detail is far from the aim of this book.

Even so, I think some degree of knowledge will help set the scene, especially for those who may have picked up a copy of this book just because they find the picture content appealing. This chapter aims to give a background of the VW story, from the early days through to the ways in which the Beetle was accepted into popular culture, and went on to be the world's bestselling single model production car.

When the KDF Wagen – Kraft Durch Freude translates literally as Strength Through Joy – was conceived, it was to provide cheap, honest transportation to the German people. The idea had existed for many years in the mind of Ferdinand Porsche, and he was determined to get it into production. At the time, in 1930s Germany, a period of depression and low-income levels following

It wasn't until the late 1940s that Ferdinand Porsche's dream, of his 'Volksauto' on every German Autobahn, came true. (Courtesy Keith Seume)

WW1 meant that car ownership wasn't the norm. Porsche's dream was to get every German family behind the wheel of a low-priced economy car.

When Adolf Hitler took notice of Porsche and his idea, Porsche had already had several false starts getting his 'Volksauto' funded and into production. Nazi propaganda required that German cars dominated the race tracks in the mid-1930s, and few people knew more about car design than Porsche. When the two met at the Hotel Kaiserhof in Berlin, Hitler showed Porsche some drawings of what he had in mind for the 'People's Car' – a four-seater family car with a one litre engine.

What followed was Porsche being put under contract by the RDA – the German car manufacturers' trade organisation – even though it clearly saw the project as a threat to its own income levels. No one, not even Hitler with his world domination fetish,

Porsche being driven in one of the VW38 prototypes; it would be ten years before the Volkswagen would go into production in German hands.
(Courtesy Keith Seume)

could have predicted how successful the Volkswagen would become globally, or how long it would stay in production.

Ferdinand Porsche's legacy

Unfortunately, Ferdinand Porsche's association with Volkswagen was not to last. After World War II had ended, the Allies considered that Porsche had done too much for Hitler – not only had he made the People's Car, but his own factory had also manufactured military material. Porsche initially spent three months in prison, under intensive questioning by British and American forces. He was then tricked into thinking that the French were taking over Wolfsburg production and was invited into talks with them. When this turned out to be false, French car manufacturers insisted Porsche be interned for alleged violations of the Hague Convention. Porsche was exonerated two years later, but by then his health was in decline, due to being imprisoned first in Baden-Baden, then in an unheated cell in Dijon.

Fortunately, Porsche did at least get to see the miracle he had always dreamed about; he was invited to Wolfsburg in September 1950 and spent the day discussing the future of the Volkswagen with Heinz Nordhoff. It is reported that upon returning to his home in Zell am See, Austria, Porsche was overcome with emotion seeing the German autobahns full of his Volkswagen, the car he had fought for so long to develop and get into production. Unfortunately, the war and subsequent

years of accusation and imprisonment had taken its toll on Porsche and the father of the VW Beetle died on January 30, 1951.

Volkswagen – back in German hands

Whilst it was Major Ivan Hirst and Colonel Charles Radclyffe of the British Army who were largely responsible for getting the bombed-out VW factory at Wolfsburg back on its feet at the end of WWII, it was the appointment of Heinrich 'Heinz' Nordhoff on January 1, 1948 that was key in the Volkswagen becoming a global success. Nordhoff recognised that, while the Volkswagen was a well-designed car, it contained a few faults and lacked many things in its present form that would appeal to global markets.

Central to Nordhoff's plans for the company was a single model approach, much like the path Henry Ford had taken with the Model T. Improved quality was very much on Nordhoff's agenda right from the very beginning, as were increased production levels.

By September 6, 1949, when the factory was entirely handed back to the Germans, Nordhoff had already managed to triple production in the first six months of that year; in May, the 50,000th Volkswagen had rolled off the production line and was celebrated by a special dinner for the workers. Quality was still a serious issue though; although the car worked, it needed serious refinement. Initially, anyone who managed to clock up 100,000 miles (62,000km) with the original engine still intact would receive a letter of congratulations and a gold watch from the factory. As quality improved, this was soon withdrawn, making those watches highly prized today.

The interior of Robert Velis' '51 Standard; compared to Export models, there are very few creature comforts.
(Courtesy Robert Velis)

Dean Bradley's '50 Export model Beetle illustrates, perfectly, the differences in trim levels compared to Robert Velis' Standard model. Chrome bumpers, horn grilles, and grooved aluminium side trim are the main outward features of the Export model, along with a wider choice of paint colours. (Author's collection)

Dean is a member of the UK chapter of the German Folks Klub: the number plate nails it perfectly. (Author's collection)

Robert Velis' '51 Standard model Beetle is a rare, all original, Survivor car, and typical of the austerity of the early Standard models. The L21 Pearl Grey paint is Patina perfection. (Courtesy Robert Velis)

Just under 50 per cent of Buses were ordered in primer as early as 1950; customers wanted the option of custom painting their vehicles, usually in company colours. (Author's collection)

The early Export dashboard is a pure art form, especially when adorned with so many accessories, as with Hans Hallen's '51 Karmann Kabriolett. This is another all-original, untouched Survivor car: note the Patina on the steering wheel and around the ignition key. (Author's collection)

Nordhoff first tackled the engine reliability issues. In June 1949 better crankcase breathing was introduced, followed by, in September that year, improvements to the metal composition of the cylinders. Roadholding was also improved from 1950, with better shock absorbers and an extra leaf in the front torsion bars.

With the most pressing issues ironed out, Nordhoff worked hard to build an Export model. Designed to appeal to demanding car buyers outside of Germany, the Export model needed some improvements in the levels of equipment and trim offered. Standard models at the time were very austere, with painted bumpers, no chrome trim, and cable-operated brakes. Wolfsburg's General Director knew that this was not a car that would appeal to global markets in its standard form; he also knew that to stand a chance of winning global sales volume, the Export model had to be right from the start. Export models not only featured hydraulic brakes, chrome bumpers, and increased levels of trim, but also a wider range of colours.

To silence criticism over excessive engine noise, Export models also had better sound deadening in the engine compartment, while, at the front of the car, the horn was moved from the bumper to under the left front wing. In order for it to still be heard, a small grille was placed in front of it, with a matching one on the opposite side. The speedometer pod was now ivory, with a new two-spoke steering wheel and optional ivory radio. Passengers could enjoy extra comfort by adding a pair of optional rear seat bolsters in the same fabric as the interior.

As early as 1950, this new Export model was being sold by New York dealer Max Hoffmann (although it was only 352 units that year), but within ten years of the end of WWII the Beetle was selling all around the world, and being produced in CKD (completely knocked down) form in many countries, including Ireland, South Africa, and Brazil.

Introducing the Transporter

While Wolfsburg was making progress with the Beetle, the introduction of a new model – the Transporter – kept the design and development team even busier. During the British Army's occupation of the factory, Major Ivan Hirst created a flatbed vehicle with a rear engine to carry parts around the huge factory. Inspired by this, Dutch importer and entrepreneur Ben Pon took the idea of the Plattenwagen to the Dutch government for approval.

When he was rejected, he approached Hirst and his superior officer, Colonel Charles Radclyffe, with a rough sketch of a newly-proposed model; the sketch was of a box-shaped body with a rear engine, capable of carrying 750kg. The idea was ultimately rejected by Radclyffe, his hands full with Beetle production at the time. A year later, however, in 1948, Pon approached the then-new General Director, Heinz Nordhoff, with the same idea. This time, the idea was well received.

Nordhoff had experience in the commercial vehicle industry, having managed Opel's lorry factory in Brandenburg in 1942 – the largest of its kind in Europe, producing 4000 vehicles per month. With such a background, Nordhoff noticed something radically different in Pon's sketch, and was the ideal man to pull off such a project. In the autumn of 1948, in cahoots

with Wolfsburg's Technical Director, Alfred Haesner, the go-ahead was given for work to begin on the design of Volkswagen's first commercial vehicle.

In line with how Nordhoff developed the Beetle, he demanded fast progress. So much so, that by November 20, 1948, the first plans were available for the new model, designated Typ 29. The design team provided two different renditions and Nordhoff chose the most aesthetically pleasing, although it was later given a more rounded front after wind tunnel testing.

The first prototypes of the Transporter featured a separate chassis, like the Beetle, but after initial testing in March/April 1949, it became obvious that the separate chassis didn't equip the vehicle with enough torsional strength. With the additional weight provided by the van body, the chassis would collapse when fully loaded; it was back to the drawing board.

Under tremendous pressure (Nordhoff had decided to begin marketing the Transporter in early 1950), Haesner set to work creating something both stronger and lighter. The result was a vehicle of unitary construction: outwardly very similar to the original, but inwardly of monocoque construction. Two longitudinal box section chassis members were used, along with outriggers and floors welded directly to the frame, which resulted in an incredibly tough and utilitarian vehicle.

When it came to getting around the obvious power deficiency from using the Beetle engine in a much heavier vehicle, it was decided to utilise the reduction gearboxes from the wartime Kübelwagen; this would increase ground clearance, while simultaneously reducing gearing, allowing a fully-loaded Transporter to climb even the steepest of hills.

Production of the Transporter (Type 2) began on March 8, 1950 at a rate of ten vehicles per day.

Top: You can clearly see the lack of rear windscreen on Gene Langan's 1950 'Südfunk' Panel Bus.
Middle: Hardcore VW Bus aficionados could tell you how many differences there are on a 1950 Bus compared to later Buses, including any number of infinitely small changes; in the last few years there have been a large number of epic restorations on Barndoor Buses, but the 'Südfunk' Bus is a very rare Survivor that has needed very little sympathetic preservation work.
Bottom: It's perhaps easier to see the lack of a front roof peak on a Barndoor Bus from the side. Note how the cargo doors have faded at a different rate to the main body, evidenced by the original logos showing in negative form. (All courtesy Gene Langan)

Early 23-window Deluxe Buses must have been a sight to behold in the austere early 1950s; John Jones' Barndoor Deluxe fell off a cliff in Moab, Utah in 1967, but he managed to skilfully repair it without affecting the incredible Patina.
(Courtesy John Jones/Kustom Coach Werks)

For many years, Alan 'Scotty' Scott's '52 RHD Barndoor Standard Microbus was believed to be the earliest RHD in existence; VW officially began producing RHD Type 2s in 1954. (Author's collection)

company livery. Of course, with the Transporter being rushed to market so quickly, the first few years of production and use highlighted many changes that needed to be made. The first of these was the addition of a rear windscreen; until November 1950, the Transporter came with a second large VW badge on the rear, in place of a window, making visibility especially poor.

The success of the T2 was pretty instant for Volkswagen, and in mid-1951 VW added the Kombi, Microbus and Deluxe Microbus to the range. Whereas the Kombi was marketed as a great multi-purpose vehicle for business owners – remove the rear seats and you had a large van – the Microbus was an entirely new concept, offering luxury trim levels, new paint colours, and a generous list of extra cost options. The Deluxe Microbus – marketed as *Sondermodell*, or Special Model – must have been an incredible sight when it debuted at the

Although most were despatched in the only colour offered by VW at the time – L31 Dove Blue – the Type 2 could also be ordered in primer. Around 45 per cent of companies buying Type 2s took advantage of this and had the vehicle painted in their own

Absolute VW's '54 Barndoor shop truck originates from Sweden; the original logos are showing through from under the peeling repaint.
(Author's collection)

Frankfurt Auto Show in April 1951, with its chrome trim, full-width dashboard, roof windows, and a huge sunroof.

In 1952, even more models came. First, the Ambulance (Type 27): created in conjunction with the German Ambulance Service, the body required substantial re-tooling at the rear to incorporate a fold-down hatch for stretchers, meaning that the engine lid also needed to be made shorter and the fuel was now filled via an external flap. These changes would eventually be incorporated into the full range in April 1955.

The last model to be launched, at least in the early years, was the Pickup, due to the body needing to be

Top: It took substantial re-tooling for Volkswagen to manufacture the Single Cab Pickup; as a result, it was the final Type 2 model made available in the 'Barndoor' years. Gene Langan's '52 'Smoothgate' truck is an incredible original Survivor.
Middle: The rear view of Gene Langan's '52 shows the smooth drop gates in all their glory; Volkswagen re-tooled in 1953 to produce stronger drop gates with built-in pressings.
Bottom: In this picture, you can clearly see the seam in the Barndoor roof pressing, as well as the smooth side gates. The passenger mirror on this truck was added later – mirrors from April 1955 onwards used an arm mounted in the door hinge, but passenger side mirrors were rarely fitted as standard until the late 1950s.
(All courtesy Gene Langan)

The Binz Double Cab was manufactured by Binz Karosserie in Germany until Volkswagen came up with the Double Cab in late 1958; it was based on the Single Cab body (note the factory bed seam on the side of the rear body), and very few survived. The Binz is easily identified by the longer rear side window than a VW-produced Double Cab, and usually has a rear-hinged 'suicide' rear door. This example was discovered in 2018. (Courtesy Kyle Golding)

radically re-designed and the new tooling produced; Volkswagen didn't have a huge contingency budget at the time and relied on sales of the existing Type 2 models before it could afford to launch new ones. The Pickup (Type 26) was a huge success for Volkswagen. Within three years, it was selling just 1000 units shy of the Kombi, which it soon overtook, making the Pickup second in sales volume to the Panel Van.

It would be a further six years before VW would add the final model to its Transporter range. The Double Cab Pickup was launched in late 1958, and was perfect for small gangs of workmen, or guys with a family who also needed a truck. Prior to Volkswagen launching its own Double Cab, coachbuilders like Binz in Germany offered their own versions, based on a modified Single Cab; these would usually have a 'suicide' rear door and a longer rear side window.

Worldwide VW dealers

Until America went Volkswagen crazy in the late 1950s, Sweden was Volkswagen's largest export market – the Beetle was out-selling all of the British exports combined. Conversely, in Britain – a nation of small-car producers – Beetle sales were minimal in the '50s; following the war, it took a brave person to be seen driving a product of Hitler's Germany. However, returning servicemen often brought VWs home to the UK, and Surrey motor trader John Colborne-Baber saw a gap in the market, taking many of these cars

Bengt Nyberg's 'Swedish Binz' was actually built by a Swedish coachbuilder, presumably to save money; it's the only one known to exist, and has undergone a full 'chassis off' restoration. (Courtesy Michael Åkerblom)

Few who'd witnessed the Volkswagen story at its conception could have imagined these cars cruising around in the early evening light in Phoenix, Arizona, 80 years later. Randy and Alicia Slack are rightly happy and proud of their '57 Karmann Cabriolet 'Burdie.' (Courtesy Andrew Thomson/AThompsonsPhoto)

Si Medlicott's 1954 Survivor Beetle was one of the first RHD cars produced at Wolfsburg. VW Motors UK was founded in 1953, and for the first time it was possible for the British to order a new RHD Volkswagen. Having owned a few lowered Patina cars, Si now prefers stock height; this car was slammed with BTR wheels, but has now been returned to original height. (Courtesy Si Medlicott)

"You can paint a lot of fun out of a car," according to Bob Van Heyst; I'm sure Si Medlicott is inclined to agree when behind the wheel of his all-original '54.
(Courtesy Si Medlicott)

Although, in recent years, replica square weave carpet sets have been made available by a few suppliers, nothing beats the Patina and wear of a set of original carpets, as on Si's Beetle.
(Courtesy Si Medlicott)

While many original cars get cosseted and locked away in private collections, Si and Jess Medlicott still use their '54 as intended. (Courtesy Si Medlicott)

in part exchange, and he soon realised the car's sales potential; in 1952, he was awarded the first franchise to sell new VWs in Britain.

However, it was Irishman Stephen O'Flaherty who acquired the UK concession in 1953, with his London-based company, VW Motors. Stephen was the man behind the Irish CKD production facility, so seemed like the obvious choice to run Volkswagen UK. Despite anti-German sentiment, there was a shortage of new cars in Britain at the time, and by late 1954, Volkswagen UK had sold 4000 cars; by 1964, just ten years later, there were 100,000 Beetles on UK roads.

By 1955, despite the opinions of concerned critics, who insisted that the same prewar design would not continue to sell in large numbers year after year, 1000 cars a day were leaving the factory, and Volkswagen realised it could never produce enough cars in one factory to fulfil worldwide demand. The 'ridiculous' Volkswagen had confounded many so-called automotive experts throughout the world and was an incredible sales success.

A coachbuilt Volkswagen sports car?

Hot on the heels of these sales successes was the launch of the VW Karmann Ghia. It was, in fact, Wilhelm Karmann Jr who was pushing for this project; Karmann already manufactured the Beetle Cabriolet, and an initial meeting between Wilhelm Karmann Sr and Nordhoff in 1950 had failed to reach a satisfactory outcome, mainly as Wolfsburg was already struggling to keep up with production demands on the Beetle.

Karmann Jr wouldn't give up on

It's rare for coachbuilt Karmann Ghias to survive in such good condition; Chris Palomba's Mango Green Ghia came from California and has incredible Patina, too. (Courtesy Joss Ashley)

the project, however, and kept bombarding Wolfsburg with a succession of designs, which would ultimately be vetoed by the Head of Development and Head of Sales and Service. When Karmann Jr met with Luigi Segre, Commercial Director at Carrozzeria Ghia in Turin, Segre made no explicit commitment to the project but decided to go ahead in secret. Segre bought a Beetle floorpan from a French VW dealer (mainly because Wolfsburg had always refused to supply one) and built a prototype, surprising Karmann Jr with it at the Paris Auto Show.

Despite the car being a Coupé (Karmann had always

Although Heinz Nordhoff was initially reluctant to progress with its own Coachbuilt car, the Karmann Ghia, with encouragement from Wilhelm Karmann Jr, several companies were already building coachbuilt versions of the Beetle; Rometsch was one such company. These cars are seriously desirable nowadays, but this didn't stop Adam Townley from keeping his Rometsch Lawrence coupe rough and ready and slamming the suspension. (Courtesy Joss Ashley)

wanted to build a convertible) he was delighted. The prototype was shipped to the Karmann factory in Osnabrück and was shown to Nordhoff and Dr Karl Feuereisen (Vice President and Head of Sales and Service) on November 16, 1954; they liked what they saw, and an agreement was made that Karmann would build the car while Volkswagen handled engineering and distribution.

The car was launched to the press on July 14, 1955. Priced at 7500DM, the car was nearly double the cost of a Standard Beetle, but considering the body was truly hand-built, the public at large didn't seem to object to the high price tag. The new Volkswagen received an astoundingly good reception; the press called the car 'beautiful' and 'high quality,' and strong sales followed. The convertible version of Karmann's dream was finally launched in 1957. Nordhoff had waited to see how the Coupé was received before committing to this more expensive model.

Volkswagen of America
The establishment of Volkswagen of America (VWoA) in 1955 was, on paper at least, an overnight success; by the end of 1955, sales had tripled the previous four years' total. Experts thought the Beetle – dubbed 'Bug' in the USA – was too primitive for US tastes, at a time when car designs were radically updated each year, all cars had V8 engines, and gas was cheap so fuel economy didn't matter. Despite this, Americans, Californians in particular, loved the little Bug and what it represented – an antithesis to the built-in obsolescence coming out of Detroit each year. Before long, Bugs and Transporters were everywhere, and

Volkswagen achieved all of this without any form of national advertising until 1959.

In next to no time, VW buyers in the USA had to wait anything up to five months to take delivery of their new car. This resulted in strong used car prices and low depreciation. The only reason that Volkswagen decided to start advertising its products, was in response to Detroit's 'Big Three' – Ford, GM and Chrysler – who, in autumn of 1959, planned to launch their own compact cars in an attempt to stem the flow of imports affecting their bottom line. Once a car that had appeared insignificant to America's motoring giants as late as 1954, the little Volkswagen had now become a major threat; as the fins and chrome craze began to wane, the little Bug and Bus piqued people's interest.

'Think Small' – VWs in advertising
With the threat of domestic compact cars, VWoA decided it was time to act, and Carl Hahn travelled to the USA. Hahn reputedly met around 4000 American advertising agencies over a period of three months, before settling on the little-known Doyle Dane Bernbach (DDB) to deliver a VW campaign. DDB had previously worked with El Al Airlines and Levis, and what followed in the subsequent VW campaign would bring the little Bug into the hearts of millions.

Whereas American car advertising at the time was brash, and made bold statements about cars making the buyer's life better, DDB spoke to the prospective car owner as if to an intelligent friend; it didn't make outlandish claims, but instead the copy was self-effacing and sincere. The ads encouraged people to 'Think Small' and get back to basics, and they worked; within two years of Detroit's compact cars launching, sales of imported cars had dropped by almost 50 per cent, but sales of the VW had actually increased, and in 1962, the company celebrated a total of one million units sold to the USA.

No one could have envisaged that the humble VW Bus would be so popular in the USA. It became such a popular economy vehicle and counter-culture icon, and the climate – especially in the western states – was so favourable, that original paint Buses, such as Robert Ramsey's Palm Green over Sand Green microbus, are still being discovered today. (Courtesy Robert Ramsey)

After we paint the car we paint the paint.

The DDB Volkswagen ad campaign was a work of true genius, and helped bestow even more character on these cars. This ad, about the quality of the factory paintwork, shows why so many VWs have made it to 40, 50, or 60 years with strong original paint. (Author's collection)

Of course, the DDB advertising wasn't entirely responsible for VWs continuing success; the compact offerings from Detroit would increase in size each year, with higher performance and more luxury, while the thrifty Volkswagen appealed to everyone as a characterful car which could be parked anywhere and would get good gas mileage.

The end of the single model policy

Nordhoff had always tirelessly worked on the one model strategy, despite pressure from others in the company and the media. He was against change for change's sake and would only make improvements to refine the car, make safety improvements, or make it better to drive. It was quite a shock to the media, then, when Volkswagen debuted the new VW 1500 range at the 1961 Frankfurt Auto Show. After years of a marketing strategy where a re-designed door handle would constitute a major model change, the Type 3 range was entirely new.

Featuring a stylish and spacious interior, ball joint front suspension, and solid front torsion bars, the Type 3 drove in a remarkably different way to the Beetle, yet still had the same configuration: an external floorpan, and a rear-mounted, air-cooled engine. The main thing that differentiated a Type 3 engine from a Beetle one, apart from the extra horsepower, was that the engine cooling fan was now attached to the rear end of the crankshaft. This meant the engine could be accommodated under the rear floor, making space for a boot/trunk in the rear as well as the front.

What this also meant is that a Variant version (named Squareback in the USA) could be added to the range in 1962, to join the Notchback and Type 3 Karmann Ghia launched in 1961. Unusually, Volkswagen had also chosen to debut a 1500 convertible at the 1961 Paris Auto Show, and had even gone as far as getting brochures made, but the convertible version never went into production. The Fastback version joined the range in 1965 and was thought by the press to be

An elaborate display, featuring the new Type 3 Saloon and Variant, marked an exciting time for VW in the early '60s. Although it featured a similar layout, the Type 3 was all-new, and a deviation from Nordhoff's single model policy. (Courtesy Keith Seume)

Chip Rodriguez bought his all-original Survivor 1963 Notchback in 1991, and he still uses it regularly, including driving it back to visit the original owners. (Courtesy 10ft_Doug)

a replacement for the now aging Beetle. Little did they know, the Beetle would go on to outlast all other air-cooled models.

A myth perpetuated by the media, and several people at Volkswagen who by this time didn't agree with Nordhoff or his policies, the Type 3 range was often reported as a flop: an unsuccessful model with poor sales. The reality couldn't be further from the truth, especially in the USA market. The Type 4, however, didn't fare quite so well; upon its launch in 1968, six months after Nordhoff's death, the press and public at large were expecting something different from Volkswagen, and the Type 4, despite being technically superior to any of the air-cooled models thus far, wasn't a sales success. This was probably due, in part, to its unusual (some would say ugly) looks.

By the time the Type 4 launched, Kurt Lotz was in charge and, despite the Type 4 being in the works since before Nordhoff's death and many regarding it as his final legacy, changes were afoot at Wolfsburg.

The end of the first golden age
Annual sales peaked in the USA in 1968, with well over half a million Bugs, Buses, Type 3s, and Karmann Ghias sold that year alone. Sadly

When Volkswagen launched the 1500S Type 3 range in August '63, with dual carburettors and more luxurious trim, the base model became the 1500N. The author's old 1966 N Squareback was a California Survivor car with some subtle suspension modifications. (Author's collection)

The Type 3 range is very easy to lower with basic hand tools and retains great ride quality. 1966 was the first year for four-lug wheels and front disc brakes; fitting Porsche Fuchs wheels requires the discs and rear hubs to be re-drilled. (Author's collection)

Steve Gilbert, of One on One Restorations, knows how to put together a great-looking car; his original paint '65 1500S Squareback drives as good as it looks, clocking up thousands of miles each year travelling to VW shows all over Europe. (Courtesy Steve Sharp)

though, from 1968, sales of new Volkswagens went into a gradual decline, not helped by the devaluation of the dollar in the early '70s, which meant that the price of a Volkswagen in US showrooms became noticeably inflated. By this point though, although sales of the Golf (Rabbit in the USA) and other VW water-cooled models began to take off, many were still happy owning and driving their reliable used Volkswagens for years, even decades, to come: such was the quality of the air-cooled cars.

Moreover, with the price of a new Volkswagen now inflated, the older used cars still held strong value with little depreciation. This was helped by Nordhoff's quest to build cars to the highest possible quality, something reflected in DDB's advertising of the period, and something which resulted in a lot of cars surviving in incredible condition, even to this day.

The Type 3 'Razor Edge' Karmann Ghia was never as popular as the Type 1, but still sold 42,000 examples in its eight years of production. Looking, for all intents and purposes, like an Italian sports car, the thin roof pillars also gave the car a look straight out of *The Jetsons*. Chadd Magee's slammed '64 was originally a UK car, but now resides in the USA. (Courtesy Alexis Peraza)

A symbol of peace

As the popularity of VW air-cooled models hit a high in 1968, the hippie movement was gathering pace, and the Volkswagen became recognised as a symbol of the peace movement. For a car conceived in Germany, championed by such an evil dictator, to end up – less

Germany was literally teeming with VWs by 1968, but sales had peaked; the air-cooled years went into decline from 1969 onwards. (Courtesy Keith Seume)

Produced at the height of Beetle production, the author's Zenith Blue 1968 Sunroof Beetle was kept by the second owner in Bavaria, Germany, from 1969 until 2013. The incredible Patina resulted from being parked outside each summer; the rust-free body condition hints that the car was stored dry in the winter. (Author's collection)

than 25 years later – becoming a symbol for world peace may seem ludicrous to some. What the VW actually represented was freedom, individuality, and two fingers up to 'The Man': a likeable alternative to the gas-guzzling offerings of America's big corporations, and a friendly-faced car with a humble reputation.

How a car went from being a symbol of Nazi Germany to being embraced the world over confounds people, even today. From its shaky beginnings, the Volkswagen also became a cult car, an icon that sold over 21 million units worldwide, and was adopted by the alternative culture in California. The VW became synonymous with surfing, young people, and the cool Californian way of life.

Synonymous with surfing

Surfers had always picked out cheap, old cars to transport their boards to the beach and far-flung destinations. Early 'Woody' Station Wagons were always a favourite, as they were very spacious inside – room for all the boards, a few girls, and the dog. When the mid-'60s arrived though, VW Bugs and Buses became cool to be seen in and were plentiful. What's more, when it came to the VW Bus, it offered more interior space than a Woody and an unburstable air-cooled engine. It could be driven in very high and very low temperatures without overheating or the engine coolant freezing.

According to Brendan Finn of Holy Grail Garage, when it came to choosing a first car in 1980s California, "Split Windshield Buses were the coolest thing you could buy for such a low price, and you could fit as many boards as you wanted in them." Although Buses were made popular by Californian surfers – several buses featured in surf films of the time, such as Bruce Brown's *Endless Summer* – they

An old 'hippie' repaint was responsible for the survival of the original paint on Tony Brown's L345 Light Grey Kombi; Tony stripped off the repaint, and discovered old, faded company logos, which he has retouched. (Courtesy Tony Brown)

Brendan Finn's old 1955 Kombi had 'the look' before many even knew what Patina was; back in 2003 when this was taken, very few people were doing Patina cars the right way. (Courtesy Brendan Finn)

Keeping your Volkswagen alive

The thing that differentiated Volkswagens from other import vehicles was the parts and service availability; from very early on, Volkswagen established a huge number of worldwide dealers, meaning that, whether you had an engine fault in Nairobi or needed brake parts in Kiruna, in the Swedish Arctic Circle, VW had you covered. There was also a wealth of independent specialists able to fix your Volkswagen if it broke down.

Not content with this network of repairers, many people wanted to fix their own Volkswagens, to keep the cost down, and be able to get home if something broke while they were on a long journey. Many repair manuals were produced by several companies worldwide, but perhaps the most famous is John Muir's *How to Keep Your Volkswagen*

were adopted the world over as cheap to run, reliable vehicles, in which you could literally cross continents: and many did.

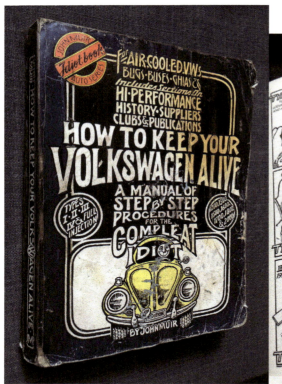

The author's well-used copy of John Muir's 'Idiot Book' – purchased in 1990, and still used as a reference today. The book sold over a million copies and is reputed to be the bestselling self-published book in history. Unlike any other car workshop manual, the Muir book speaks in a language anyone can understand, and the diagrams by Peter Aschwanden made the author confident to 'have a go' at a young age. It isn't just a great workshop manual; the many drawings by Aschwanden, and Muir's laid-back writing style make it a fun read.
(All author's collection)

Alive: A Manual of Step-By-Step Procedures for the Compleat Idiot. John was an aeronautical engineer, who decided to drop out, '60s style, grow his hair long, and write the definitive guide to fixing the Volkswagen for people of all knowledge levels.

The book was illustrated by artist Peter Aschwanden and was self-published in 1969. It sold more than two million copies, and became one of the most successful self-published books in history. It's a delight to read, even if you're not into repairing Volkswagens; the illustrations by Aschwanden and the friendly, simple tone of the book make reading it a joy, unlike most other technical publications.

I can clearly remember ordering my first copy in 1990, aged 15, eager to buy an old VW. The book taught me to 'have a go,' and to not be scared of delving into the workings of my first Beetle, which I bought a year later. This ultimately led to me running a VW workshop for several years and writing my own

technical 'How-To' articles for VW magazines, still to this day. As of 2018, the book is still available new. After Muir's death in 1977, it was then updated by Tosh Gregg and is now on its 19th edition.

The aftermarket VW parts and labour industry also continues; I don't think there is a make of classic cars today that has greater availability of spares or restoration parts. The only issue is the quality of some of the aftermarket parts themselves – quite often it's better to try to source a genuine, 50-year-old Volkswagen part that has lasted well and still has many years left in it, than to take a chance with a new aftermarket part.

Whatever the quality of parts though, it's safe to say that hundreds of thousands of classic VWs wouldn't still be on the road without them. Even in the last ten to 15 years, the quality of repair panels has increased tremendously, to the point that it is now possible to restore Bugs, Buses and other models that, ten years ago, most would think were only fit for spares.

Modifying Volkswagens

With the huge stateside car culture, especially in California, it was only a matter of time before Volkswagens would start to be modified in people's backyards. This was helped, in part, by Joe Vittone, who founded the Economotors Volkswagen dealership in Riverside, California in 1954. Economotors was one of the earliest VW dealers in California, and was one of the most successful, but Joe soon discovered an issue with the cylinder heads, which caused the valve guides to wear out at relatively low mileage. There were no parts from Volkswagen to repair this at the time; Volkswagen would advise the owner to discard the cylinder head and replace with a new one. Joe saw a gap in the market and decided to manufacture his own valve guides, which enabled cars to be repaired at a much lower cost, without discarding the original cylinder heads.

The valve guides sold very well, and became a very profitable sideline to the Economotors dealership, leading Joe to found European Motor Products Inc (EMPI) in 1956. By the mid-'50s, the automotive performance scene was really taking off in the USA, with the majority of Detroit's manufacturers offering high-performance versions of their regular production cars; Chevrolet's introduction of the small block V8 engine into the Tri-Chevy line (1955-57) led the way. Although many Volkswagen owners decided to buy a Volkswagen because they were economical, the main complaint from owners at the time was that their cars lacked power, at least when compared with anything offered by Detroit.

Getting more out of the Volkswagen

In 1956, EMPI added Okrasa parts to the range, enabling VW owners to hike the power by up to 50 per cent. This was followed by the addition of Denzel products, from Austria, in 1958; they were more expensive than Okrasa parts, but of a much higher quality. Of course, making the VW go quicker was no good if the car became unmanageable on twisty roads, so in 1958 EMPI introduced a front sway bar – something which Volkswagen adopted just one year later. In fact, the heavier Karmann Ghia had been fitted with one since its inception.

With the front suspension taken care of in the handling department, Vittone could turn his attention towards the rear suspension. Early swing axle Volkswagens and Porsches (and the 1960-64 Chevrolet Corvair) had always suffered from the inner rear wheel tucking under during hard cornering, resulting in often dangerous oversteer and single car crashes. EMPI launched the Camber Compensator, a device that bolted to the rear-mounted transaxle, complete with limiting straps for the rear axle tubes. This transformed the handling of swing axle cars and, combined with a front sway bar, made VWs capable enough to enter into performance events and racing.

The fitment of a Camber Compensator to EMPI's own 1956 Beetle, enabled it, along with racing driver Dan Gurney, to go out and win the 1963 Grand Prix of Volkswagens in Nassau. By now, the 'E' of EMPI had changed from 'European' to 'Engineered,' as Vittone felt it suggested a greater emphasis on product development. The Camber Compensator and front sway bar, made famous by Gurney's 1963 win, went on to sell more than 100,000 units worldwide; units were also manufactured in the UK by world champion Graham Hill's company Speedwell.

The issue with swing axle suspension was made public in the 1966 book *Unsafe at Any Speed* by Ralph Nader, who campaigned for many car manufacturers to correct the in-built safety issues found in cars being

The EMPI Inch Pincher developed out of the old Nassau-winning Oval Window car, and was responsible for winning many David and Goliath style battles with big, American V8 cars.
(Courtesy Keith Seume)

produced at the time. Ultimately, all car manufacturers re-designed their products: Chevrolet fitted a transverse-mounted rear spring to correct the handling of the Corvair in 1964, and Volkswagen fitted re-designed rear torsion bars and a rear handling bar for 1967 models. Both manufacturers fitted completely re-designed and fully independent rear suspension in the next few years. All Volkswagens destined for the USA market were fitted with IRS rear suspension from 1969 onwards, while in Europe and other markets, swing axle cars continued to be sold.

New parts continued to be launched by EMPI, including steel 'Sprint Star' wheels. There were collaborations with the aforementioned Speedwell, as well as with Tony Rudd at BRM (to manufacture the now famous BRM wheel), and Chris Shorrock, manufacturer of the Shorrock Supercharger kits. Before parts could be added to the range, Head of R&D, Dean Lowry, would develop them on the Grand Prix-winning 1956 Bug, which morphed into the 'Inch Pincher' drag race car. The company soon became world famous for

producing performance VW parts, especially when the Inch Pincher would go on to win David and Goliath style battles against powerful V8 cars.

Being in the unique position of owning both a Volkswagen dealership and an aftermarket performance parts company, Vittone decided, in 1966, to introduce new cars off the showroom floor, fitted

The original EMPI Sprint Star wheel – such as this one in Danny Zepeda's collection – was much revered, and available in chromed or painted finish. BBT in Belgium now reproduces the wheel in steel as original. (Courtesy Julien-David Collombet/ *Super VW* Magazine)

Original EMPI GTV cars are now very rare, original paint ones even more scarce; Andy Fleet's '72 was involved in a bad accident years ago, but he sympathetically restored the car, only blending in Texas Yellow paint where needed. (Author's collection)

Winning at Nassau put EMPI, especially the rear Camber Compensator handling device, on the map; the company went on to sell 100,000 examples. (Courtesy Keith Seume)

Father and son, Jon and Danny Heeley, are both into Patina VWs in a big way. Danny's car is an original Texas Yellow EMPI GTV but this picture also shows the later four-lug EMPI Sprint Star wheels, chromed on Jon's Squareback and with a painted finish on Danny's GTV. (Courtesy Jon Heeley)

with a full range of EMPI parts, but still covered by a full warranty. These cars, known as EMPI GTVs, were available in four levels of equipment, priced from just $437 over the standard car. This helped EMPI to expand across the USA, with no fewer than 28 distributors and an incredible 489 agents spread throughout 43 states. At its peak, EMPI sold up to $6 million worth of parts each year, before being sold to Filter Dynamics in 1971.

Some of the original team behind EMPI decided to leave and set up their own companies from the late '60s onwards: Vittone's son Darrell left to form The Race Shop, and Dean Lowry left to build engines full time, forming Deano Dyno-Soars with his brother Ken. By this point, the performance VW industry and VW drag racing were in a boom period,

Danny Heeley's original paint EMPI GTV is mildly lowered with a two-inch narrowed front beam and drop spindles, but retains original EMPI Sprint Star wheels – 4.5in wide in front and 5.5in wide at the rear. (Courtesy Danny Heeley)

with the first Bug-In VW drag racing show being held in 1968. Until Bug-In, there were no specific VW-only drag race events; owners of drag race VWs would have to attend all-models race events around the USA.

VW shows & the buggy boom

Organised by entrepreneur Vic Wilson, the Bug-Ins would go on to be incredibly successful, and were definitely the inspiration behind the many copycat events that make the worldwide VW scene what it is today. These events showed people what was out there when it came to modifying Volkswagens, and inspired them to make changes to their cars in time for the next meeting, with the hope of coming away with a trophy or magazine feature.

As well as performance VW Bugs, dune buggies also became commonplace. People had realised the off-road potential of the VW Bug as early as the late 1950s – some would cut down the front and rear suspension of Bugs and fit wider wheels and big tyres. Being rear engined, the Bug would do well on sand and rough terrain. This is how the Baja Bug was born, and some even removed the somewhat heavy Bug bodyshell and made a sand rail out of the VW floorpan.

In 1963, California surfer, artist, engineer, and boat builder Bruce Meyers designed a fibreglass buggy bodyshell, making the first street-legal VW Buggy. Drawing on his experience in sailboat construction, Meyers personally modelled, moulded, and built 'Old Red,' which he still owns today. Initially designed for desert racing, the first 12 examples of the Meyers Manx, produced by Meyers himself, were of monocoque construction until he realised the car would be much more cost effective by making a body that would fit onto a shortened VW floorpan.

The car dominated dune racing events immediately, due to its light weight and the superior traction of the VW or Corvair rear engine, paired with a VW transaxle. In the car's first event, Meyers and his co-driver knocked four hours off the Ensenada-La Paz off-road racing record of 39 hours, leading to years of Meyers Manx domination in off-road events, and the formation of NORRA (National Off-Road Racing Association).

The Manx received worldwide acclaim when it defeated motorcycles, trucks and other vehicles to win the inaugural 1967 Mexican 1000 race (the predecessor of the Baja 1000). Throughout the late '60s, around 6000 original Meyers Manx Buggy bodies were produced, but as the design became popular,

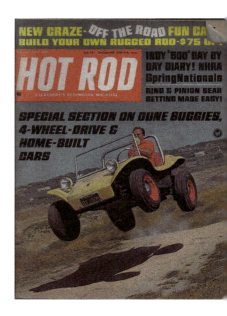

The August 1966 cover of *Hot Rod* magazine featured Bruce Meyers in flight in one of the original 12 monocoque-constructed Meyers Manx dune buggies. Meyers produced only 6000 original Manx kits (to be fitted to a shortened Beetle floorpan), but it's estimated over 250,000 copies were made worldwide after Meyers lost his patent in court. (Courtesy *Hot Rod* magazine)

many copies were produced (estimated to be around 250,000 worldwide). Although Meyers patented the design, Meyers & Co lost in court to the copiers, the judge rescinding his patent as 'unpatentable,' opening the floodgates to the industry he created.

One early copier was the Imp, produced by EMPI. Despite re-designing the Manx into the MkII, and diversifying to produce the Tow'd, Manx SR, and other variants, Bruce Meyers left the company and it ceased operation in 1971. In 2000, capitalising

Organised by entrepreneur Vic Wilson, the first Bug-In show was held in 1968. Bug-In 31 was to be the last show in 1983, due to the closure of Orange County International Raceway. Rich Kimball resurrected the show in 2007 at a new venue, and Bug-In would set the format for many of today's VW shows. (Courtesy Keith Seume)

The author's copy of Keith Seume's *VW Beetle: The New Custom Handbook*,' pricing up an original 'Old Red' style Meyers Manx buggy build during the renewed Manx fever in the early 2000s. (Author's collection)

Patina Buggies exist and can usually be picked up fairly cheaply; the fibreglass often doesn't stand the test of time too well, but Rusty Willey's buggy of unknown manufacture has survived pretty well. (Author's collection)

The buggy boom in the late '60s caught on all over the world. Companies such as GP in the UK, fielded similar designs, and it was thought of as a good way to resurrect a tired or often rusty Beetle. The boom years were undoubtedly helped by Beach Buggies in popular culture, such as featuring in Elvis Presley films, and in the original 1968 version of *The Thomas Crown Affair*, in which Steve McQueen drives a Meyers Manx equipped with a Corvair flat-six engine.

The VW club scene

Whatever the model or configuration, VW popularity was at an all-time high in the late '60s, and the emergence of countless aftermarket parts, VW shows, and a wider VW social scene was a byproduct of this. Countless performance VW clubs were launched in Southern California, the most famous of these being Der Kleiner Panzers (DKP), which worked on an invitation-only basis and were very precious about their reputation. For example, if club cars had any body damage they were not allowed to be displayed at shows until they were repaired. Many of the clubs would fight it out in a good-natured way at VW drag meets and car shows.

Despite undergoing many changes, DKP still exists today and contains many of the original members, mainly thanks to Keith Seume's California Look 'bible' – *California Look VW* – launched in 1992, in which Keith explored the entire VW performance scene in the late '60s and early '70s, reinvigorating original members by providing worldwide awareness of the era.

One member of DKP who was particularly influential in the VW scene in the late '60s was Greg Aronson. He built a white 1963 sunroof Bug with a big engine and nose-down stance, complete with a set of BRM wheels; the car was very different from what most were building at the time. A few things set Greg's car apart from its contemporaries: Greg decided to lower the front suspension with a Select-A-Drop device fitted to the front axle beam when most club members' cars at the time featured raised suspension. Lowering the front suspension was to become commonplace in drag race VWs to aid stability, but Greg's was the first streetcar to be given the treatment.

on the wave of nostalgia in France over the original Manx, Bruce Meyers formed Meyers Manx Inc to once again sell official Meyers Manx kits. He continued to produce these and newer designs well into his 90s.

Late '60s California was responsible for the VW scene as we know it today; many clubs – such as Der Kleiner Panzers (pictured) – fought for top honours at Bug-In and in VW drag racing. (Courtesy Keith Seume)

Greg Aronson's car, with its lowered front suspension and welded-up body trim holes, had thousands of copiers across the globe. (Courtesy Keith Seume/Ron Fleming)

Left to Right: Mark Thurber, Greg Aronson and Ron Fleming – the F, A and T of FAT Performance posing in front of Aronson's ground-breaking car. (Courtesy Keith Seume/ Ron Fleming)

Roof chops were never commonplace, but Mike Martinez' (pictured) and Keith Goss' car – later owned by Keith Seume – were two fine examples. Note the VW Bus in the background, customised in true 1970s 'vanning' style. Little did people know that original paint would be valued in the future. (Courtesy Keith Seume)

Nose-down suspension and de-chromed bodywork became popular in the early 1970s, leading to Jere Aldaheff coining the phrase 'The California Look' in the February 1975 issue of *Dune Buggies* and *Hot VWs* magazine. (Courtesy Keith Seume)

The birth of California Look

As well as lowering the front suspension of his car, Greg took his Bug along to Becker's Bug House in Orange, California, where he had all 49 body trim holes welded up, before having the body painted in 1968 Chevrolet truck white, which gave a stark contrast against the black sunroof cover and interior. Aronson built the car just to be different, but what followed wrote both him and the car into VW folklore. Ironically for Greg, it wasn't until the car was sold (to fellow club member Jim Holmes) that it was featured in the now iconic February 1975 issue of *Dune Buggies and Hot VWs*, when the magazine's Jere Aldaheff coined the phrase 'The California Look,' making the whole VW world want to build cars just like it.

At the time, in both California and the rest of the USA, the craze of raising suspensions on cars and vans, painting them in metallic shades, and adding stripes and accessories was commonplace. Indeed, many buses fell victim to this, having their rear wheelarches cut out in order to add wide wheels and

For many of the VW enthusiasts who got into this hobby in the 1980s, pictures like this of a smoothed-out Cal Look VW driving in the California sunsets were as good as it gets. A car built in this style would still be popular today, and the California Look style still has a huge global following, thanks in a large part to Keith Seume's California Look books. (Courtesy Keith Seume)

tyres, often from American muscle cars, and fitted with wheel adaptors. Interiors would be awash with shag-pile carpets, buttoned dralon and velour, so when California Look came about, it was hugely refreshing to many and helped to set a trend that survived through the '80s and '90s, and beyond VWs to many other brands of car.

There were similar developments happening in the Hot Rod and custom car scene too; people were catching on to subtle, understated car modifications, and many different types of cars were given the look by removing factory trim, thus simplifying the lines.

Despite Volkswagen gradually phasing out the Beetle in the late Type 3s (after the introduction of several front engined, front-wheel drive and water-cooled models), air-cooled Volkswagen fever would continue to grip the world, and does so even to this day: long may it continue.

CHAPTER TWO

In the beginning

Rat Rods to Rat Look & the Hoodride phenomenon

As with most things considered cool in the automotive world, it's generally accepted that car customising began in Southern California in the 1930s. Guys began by stripping off all the superfluous parts to make cars (usually Ford Model T, A, or B roadsters which were cheaper to buy and lighter than sedan models) go faster. Fenders and convertible tops were removed, wheels were changed, engines were tuned up, and many of these cars ran open exhaust systems, all designed to make them run faster at the dry lakes northeast of Los Angeles.

The scene really began to take off after World War II: servicemen returned from the war with new skills from their time in the military; there were cheap cars to customise; and many disused airstrips that had been built for the war effort were now sitting empty. They were ideal for repurposing into drag strips and the popularity of drag racing increased.

With this, magazines such as *Hot Rod* and *Car*

Stripping off fenders, running boards, and any extra parts, as with this '32 Ford Pickup, was the easiest way to make cars go faster in the '30s when car customising began. (Courtesy Derek 'Boxrod' Campbell)

Craft were published, to cater for this new breed of young 'Hot Rodders.' Most elders at the time thought it subversive, due to many of the early 'Hot Rods' being stolen cars that were repainted to disguise them. There was also the question of excessive speed, and the many accidents and deaths that occurred as a result.

Car magazines

When car magazines began featuring these cars, it was usually the brightly painted 'finished' cars that got all the attention, but in thousands of backyards and garages, work-in-progress Hot Rods were being built and driven hard. Although 'Rat Rod' and other similar terms were coined much, much later, there was never a time when cars weren't being driven in an unfinished state, often with bare metal or primer showing – it's just that these cars were never featured in magazines, or in popular culture.

As the decades passed and the cheap used cars available became more modern, the magazines followed suit and featured the 'Street Rods' and custom cars, too. After a while, a counterculture emerged, where people deliberately chose to run a primered or unfinished car, rather than opt for shiny paint, although it took a long time for magazines and the media to take note of this movement.

Perhaps it was because the car magazines have always felt that they need to show aspirational cars, and, for many, Patina cars don't fit into that bracket – there are even people to this day that believe owning a Patina car is a sign of laziness, not a conscious choice. Finally, as far as car magazines were concerned, in the December 1972 issue of *Rod & Custom*, 'Beaters' were first mentioned, in response to the proliferation of unfinished looking cars on the scene.

Rat Rods

There will always be disputes as to where and when the term 'Rat Rod' was coined, but many believe it was Gray Baskerville, in *Hot Rod* magazine, who made comments about cars that were left covered in primer spots year after year being Rat Rods: one such car was the '32 Ford Roadster owned by famous Hot Rod artist Robert Williams.

By 1987, when famous Hot Rodder Jim 'Jake' Jacobs created the 'Jakelopy' – a car thrown together in less than 28 days from spare parts – the mainstream Rat Rod culture was being born. Jake drove his unfinished and unpainted car into the Goodguys annual West Coast Nationals and parked it in the middle of the

Patina has always been a counterculture thing. It was often seen as the cheapest way to build a car, but there's something about a car with original Patina that makes it more special: the car's story hasn't been erased by restoration. (Courtesy Derek 'Boxrod' Campbell)

The 'Jakelopy,' painted by hand at the Goodguys West Coast Nationals in 1987. Many felt that this car promoted recognition of Rat Rods, helped by Gray Baskerville coining the phrase in *Hot Rod* magazine. (Author's collection)

A book that inspired a generation of VW enthusiasts, especially in the UK; Colin Burnham's *Air-Cooled Volkswagens* brought the '80s Cal Look craze to Europe. (Author's collection)

In the '80s, Cal Look was all about de-chromed cars with pastel coloured paint; dechroming and simplifying caught on with other types of cars. (Author's collection)

Hi-Tech category, a moment that would change the Hot Rod world; he unpacked some red paint and brushes and began to paint the car in the middle of the show. The car quickly drew a crowd and many began to pick up paintbrushes and help Jake paint his Rat Rod.

Many in the Hot Rod scene were already beginning to shy away from the shiny, higher-priced Street Rods and custom cars being featured in magazines at the time, and began to build cars that harked back to the grassroots of Hot Rodding.

The only problem, then – as it is now – was that for every traditional, well thought out Hot Rod or Rat Rod being built, there were ten unsafe cars being thrown together, usually by guys who were new to the scene, couldn't weld, had little knowledge of cars and style, and were building cars purely for a reaction, or to upset the purists. Cars began turning up at shows with rope, spikes, bullets, grenades, and plastic rats attached – cars built with little or no effort and with zero sense of flow.

Modified Volkswagens

At this point in the mid to late 1980s, the global VW scene was pretty different from the Hot Rod scene. Sure, there were unfinished cars around, with primer paint etc, but the average VW wasn't even old enough at this point to have anything you could really call Patina, and it was certainly never mentioned in the US VW magazines, *Hot VWs* and *VW Trends*; if a car had old, worn paint, then it was generally deemed to be a project car, or in need of a paint job. Cars like this would occasionally pop up in magazine car show reports, but even then it would usually only be if it was a rare or special car, and the caption would reflect that it was 'unfinished.'

Although modifying VWs had become popular in California in the late '60s, it really took a couple of decades for this to filter over to Europe, and the trends were very much reflected by what was going on in California. By 1986, the 'New Wave' VW scene in the UK was just beginning. Like their 1930s US counterparts, VWs were now being stripped of chrome and superfluous parts and being brightly

Burnham's first book brought about a Porsche-inspired Targa top craze in the UK, thanks to this car. It was pictured in the book with no owner credit, but it belonged to Luis Ruiz from Palmdale, who was reputedly also the first person to put 'alloys' (Porsche Fuchs) on a 23-window Bus – a '57. (Courtesy Colin Burnham)

painted. Performance engines were less common at this point, but engine detailing was a necessary part of the look.

Readers of *Street Machine* and *Custom Car* magazines in the UK were being drip-fed images of cool, lowered, and brightly painted 'Cal Look' VWs from California, with the occasional UK VW thrown into the mix. The big game changer for a lot of people was the serialisation of Colin Burnham's Cal Look Beetle build in *Street Machine* magazine, throughout 1986, followed by his 1986 book: *Air-Cooled Volkswagens*. Colin was the Features Editor of *Street Machine* and book sales were offered through the magazine. The book was an amazing technicolour

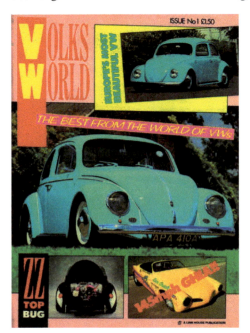

The first *VolksWorld* cover; to readers of *Street Machine, Custom Car* and *VW Motoring* at the time, *VolksWorld* was a true revelation and a really exciting time in history. (Author's collection)

feast: 128 pages packed with colourful images. I can clearly remember wearing out my first copy from reading it so much and having to buy a second one – this second, also worn, copy still takes pride of place on my bookshelf.

The UK look

June 1987 saw the first annual Bug Jam being held at Santa Pod Raceway in the UK. In a style very similar to the California Bug-In shows, the original Bug Jam was a one day show, with drag racing, show and shine (concours), and a bikini contest. In his book, *Bug Jam and All That,* show organiser Brett Hawksbee speaks of his trepidation when the gates opened for the first time, but how the show soon filled with UK 'Cal Lookers.' The UK New Wave VW scene had arrived.

VolksWorld magazine was launched in the UK in late 1987, with Keith Seume (Editor of *Custom Car* magazine) being the founder. The first few issues were full of brightly painted and fully restored (although often crudely under the surface) cars, and if anything was printed in the magazine with primer or rust, it was definitely the 'before' part of the before and after transformation. The magazine was so popular, that it went from a one-off to a quarterly, then to monthly in a short space of time.

At the time, if a VW had rust or primer spots, it was because the owner hadn't got around to restoring it yet. Even when cars were discovered as all original one-owner cars – which would only need cleaning, polishing and re-commissioning – they were still stripped down and given a full repaint.

Before long, especially in the USA, UK, and France, the vast majority of cars at any given VW show, had

UK-based Andy 'Spike' Finch lusted after Dennis Hyde's Porsche Magenta Karmann Ghia so much when he first saw it in Colin Burnham's *Air-Cooled Volkswagens* in the 1980s that he built his own pink Karmann Ghia. Four decades later, he managed to buy the original from Dennis and ship it to the UK; Although the car still looked good, Andy stripped and repainted most of the car with his patented 'Mile-deep' shine. (Author's collection)

been given this updated form of the California Look. It was a time where you could let your imagination run wild: come up with a new modification, try to find a way to fit a set of wheels that nobody had used before, or be the first to paint a car a certain colour.

Thinking back to the mid-'80s, when I got into Volkswagens, there really was no limit to the imaginations of car builders. The original Cal Look blueprint, featuring smoothed out cars with any superfluous trim removed, was refined into the UK or European Cal Look, which involved cars often undergoing more body modifications.

People would replace the original rear vents with a panel with the car's name, or other arty things cut into them, some would fit 'suicide' doors, make bumpers fit the body lines of the car better and relocate lights into them. Colin Burnham's book, *Air-cooled Volkswagens*, was largely responsible for what became a Targa top craze; Porsche had created a removable Targa roof section as far back as 1968, but Burnham's book

featured a pastel painted 1967 Bug with a homebrew Targa top section.

Before long, companies such as Thump! Thump! in the UK, run by Jay Townsend and Gary Constable, and The Paintbox, run by Simon Emery, had begun to make Targa roof conversions for customers. By this time, people were lowering the rear suspension too, and copies of the EMPI eight-spoke wheel were commonplace, although some people chose to re-drill the bolt pattern of the brake drums to run Porsche Fuchs wheels. Others, wishing to be different from anyone else, would fit billet alloy wheels or wheels from other manufacturers; in the UK, Ford Escort and Peugeot 205 wheels became popular – fully polished, of course.

Lots of New Wave VW shows, imitating Bug Jam, began springing up, especially in the UK and France. These were covered in *VolksWorld*, where lots of new companies were also advertising, to feed the car owners anything from restoration services, to upholstery, and surf-style VW branded clothing.

Since the beginning of the New Wave VW scene in Europe in the mid-1980s, there had been an explosion in prices of the faithful VW Beetle. Almost overnight, Beetles had become fashionable, and a huge industry had formed around the supply and restoration of them. Being a regular attendee at VW shows and local car cruise nights around this time – despite being too young to drive – I learned that the only VW that was more expensive than a Beetle was a VW Karmann Ghia. If you turned up at a show or cruise in a Ghia, you were considered lucky or wealthy or both.

Other VW models, such as Buses/Campers or the Type 3 range, were much slower to catch on. Sure, there would be Campers at VW shows, but most of these would be borrowed from parents and would generally be stock height and completely unmodified.

This began to change when VW shows in Europe deviated from the one-day format the USA followed. Shows in Europe, even from the early days, became full weekend shows. Promoters of these events realised that they could make more money by renting a venue for a whole weekend and putting on some camping and evening entertainment. In Europe, many of them were also at drag strips, adding a further attraction for show-goers. What shows like this did, was make people realise that having a Beetle and sleeping in a tent was actually inferior to bringing a VW Camper and having somewhere comfortable to sleep.

Cheap Buses
In the UK magazines, pictures of Split Screen VW Buses that had been lowered out in California and brightly painted helped to attract people to Type 2 ownership. Companies like Bus Boys in California were offering kits to lower Bus suspension, and Richard 'Ritchie' King, a pioneer and proprietor of the German Car Company in Southend-on-Sea, UK, began to import the Bus lowering parts and fit them to his own Buses.

Although Split Screen Buses were most popular, this was often because they were much cheaper. I recall several examples of Split Screen Buses, in good overall and roadworthy condition, being in the classifieds section of every magazine, often for around £600 to £1000. Bay Window Buses were only around ten to 15 years old at the time, so usually commanded higher prices. Ritchie himself built what I believe to be the first lowered Cal Look Bay Window Bus in the UK – the German Car Company's 'Death Bus.' Magazine pictures of a cool, well-built Bus were enough to inspire many to pick up a cheap VW Camper and build something similar; a rainy show weekend in a tent was also reason enough.

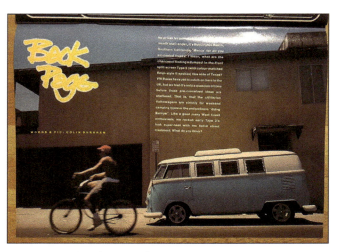

Pictures like this one from Colin Burnham on *Street Machine* magazine's 'Back Page,' helped to show thousands of car guys how cool a VW Bus could look. VW shows that lasted an entire weekend also helped the Bus craze take off in the UK.
(Author's collection)

Type 3 popularity
Type 3 models were largely absent at VW shows, until a few people, likely priced out of buying a Beetle, began to think outside the box and build Notchbacks, Fastbacks or Squarebacks. Gary Constable was one early Type 3 innovator; his Fastback was given the full '80s Cal Look treatment, lowered and smoothed with graphic paint, and cool, detailed Pedrini wheels. The car appeared in magazines and on TV in the UK.

Keith Seume also did a lot for the Type 3 popularity in the UK when he bought an orange 1972 Fastback, in good original condition, for £100, and serialised the build in *Custom Car* and *VolksWorld* magazines.

Cars like these showed people that there was more than one way to build a cool car, and also that it was possible to build a car on a low budget and still look cool at a show. Let's face it, back then, much like now, the average person getting into VWs wasn't rich and didn't possess the skills to build show worthy cars. These budget builds showed people not only to think outside the box when it came to other models, but also to realise that a good original car with a lowering job and some nice wheels could also be a cool driver.

Classic Volkswagens
At the height of this trend came another book from Colin Burnham: *Classic Volkswagens*. Whereas *Air-Cooled Volkswagens* focused on the custom VW scene, *Classic Volkswagens* focused on the history of the VW, and largely perfectly-restored, completely standard,

In 1988, Colin Burnham's second book, *Classic Volkswagens*, packed with all types of stock air-cooled Volkswagens, showed VW enthusiasts that modifying cars wasn't necessarily the way forward. Selling 250,000 copies worldwide, this book can be credited, more than anything else, for driving people to value originality when it comes to Volkswagens. (Author's collection)

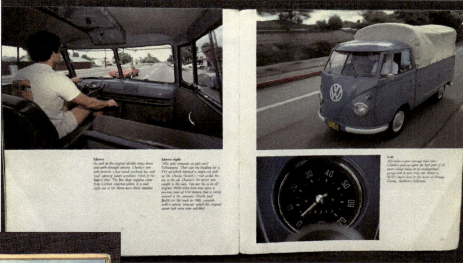

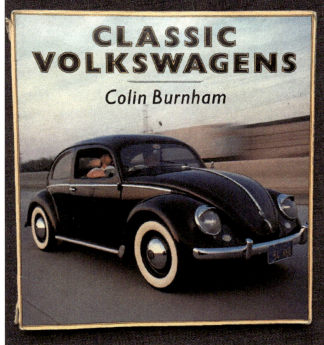

air-cooled Volkswagens of all types. The book was an instant hit; it went on to sell over 250,000 copies and was reputedly the bestselling automotive book of all time.

The second offering from Burnham had the same effect on the VW scene as the first one had. Whilst lowered suspension and aftermarket wheels appeared to be here to stay, cars started showing up at VW shows with all the original chrome trim fitted, or in some cases refitted, to show cars. 'Resto Cal' was born and the scene began to evolve again; there were even more choices when it came to customising a VW and remaining 'on trend.' As the '80s ended and the '90s gathered pace, certain people in the VW scene began

to tire of dayglo paint schemes and cars that had been de-chromed; original paint colours began to emerge back onto the scene.

Old School Cal Look

Keith Seume launched a few of his own books; notably, 1992's *California Look VW*. Where many had been stuck in a world of pastel colours and smooth bodywork, Keith's book ignited a new flame in the VW world; for the first time, many could see the bloodlines of the early days of modifying VWs, and the beginnings of Cal Look VWs, which also made it clear how wayward the 'UK Look' had become.

When Keith's book came out, both he and *VolksWorld* deputy at the time, Ivan McCutcheon, were giving readers regular doses of traditional Cal Look and what became known as 'Old School' Cal Look. Keith had managed to buy an ex-California show car – a chop-top Bug built by DKP member Keith Goss in 1976 – and Ivan had a rust-free UK '67 Beetle that had BRM wheels and a 2007cc engine.

Large displacement and powerful engines weren't really that popular in Europe at the time, with many choosing to simply dress the engine up with some chrome parts and paint detailing. Keith's book, along with *VolksWorld* and other magazines like *Super VW* in France, got everyone in Europe into high-performance VWs and nose-down suspension. A small handful of people were also beginning to narrow the front axle beams of cars, mainly so that aftermarket wheels and disc brakes would fit inside the front wheelarches.

Don't be fooled, though, into thinking that VW shows were full of show quality cars; as a regular show visitor over the years, I remember just as many project cars as finished show cars, and it was the former that

I always remember being drawn to. Like the appeal of peeling paint on the shutters of an old French house, the genuine, unspoiled Patina of an unmolested Beetle or Split Screen Camper was so attractive.

Patina VW imports

As the demand for good cars was outstripping supply, especially in the UK, people began to import cars from Europe and the USA. Countries such as Portugal and Sweden suddenly became popular spots for buying old VWs, as they seemed to be in plentiful supply, and often in much better shape than their UK counterparts.

Many of these imports became the subject of full restorations, but a fair few were deemed good enough to use as is, usually with a simple lowering job, a narrowed front beam, and a set of aftermarket wheels. A good number of these cars were still proudly wearing their original, then 30-year-old, factory paint: sometimes virtually perfect, other times sun-bleached or rust-stained. People were beginning to value originality, and these cars were as original as you could get.

VolksWorld magazine, unlike *Hot VWs* and *VW Trends* in the USA, began to notice these original cars. Before long, VW magazine show reports featured pictures of these cars and their popularity grew. As far as I can recollect, it was *VolksWorld* staff member Paul Knight (later Editor of *Ultra VW* and now Editor of *VWt* magazine) who coined the term 'Rat Look,' in relation to the Linde Bus, originally found by Ernst Bernsteiner in Vienna.

Keith Seume's 1992 book, *California Look VW,* became a bible for many; it showed readers the way cars were modified in the 1960s and '70s in California, and inspired a new Old School Cal Look craze. Former editor of *VolksWorld* Ivan McCutcheon owned this '67 Beetle (featured in Keith's book) for longer than the original owner he purchased it from. A true piece of VW scene history, the car is now owned by Jim Dix. (Courtesy Jim Dix)

Here was a magazine-featured Split Screen Panel Bus, which was lowered, had aftermarket wheels, a powerful engine, and lots of rust. A good number of readers were up in arms that such a rusty vehicle could be given a full feature in a magazine as prestigious as *VolksWorld*, but for many others, it was the beginning of enlightenment. It was also the very beginning of the Beetle losing out on popularity and value to the VW Bus.

Turning tides

Thousands of people, who had neither the time nor the budget to build a magazine-worthy show car, were now realising that they could build a cool car on a very low budget. Many of these people realised that the Linde Bus, whilst it looked rusty and rotten, was actually a pretty solid vehicle with a heavy dose of Patina covering the surface. Just as many were now also

imagining their own version of a Rat Look car, which involved junkyard-worthy wrecks of cars, with heavily lowered suspension, and nice wheels. Whilst narrowed front beams had originally come about in order to fit wider wheels inside the wheelarches, having wheels tucked in further and further was now a big part of the look, especially on Resto Cal and Patina cars.

Of course, at this point, Patina was still a counter-culture thing. Paul Knight: "I couldn't say for sure if I coined the 'Rat Look' phrase, but I know that it was me pushing to get these cars featured, and this was part of the reason I left [*VolksWorld*] to start *Ultra* [*VW*], so I could feature everything, not just shiny cars."

One of the early cars that *Ultra VW* featured was Andy Ham's self-named 'The Bitch,' a RHD '59 Beetle, which had been subjected to a full body-off restoration underneath, but proudly wore its original paint, with Patina by the truckload, a heavily narrowed front

Chris Nott's UK RHD '59 Beetle 'The Bitch' was famously built by Andy Ham; Andy showcased the build on the Restowagen UK forums, and it was featured on the cover of *Ultra VW* magazine in 2003. It is the first known car in the UK to be given a body-off restoration whilst keeping the Patina paint. (Courtesy Chris Nott)

'Money' Mike Hodgson's slammed '58 Kombi, was a landmark in the Patina VW scene; Brendan Finn was there to witness it being lowered off the jack by George Schmidt of The Butcher Shop in Visalia, California. This was the first ever Bus to have the front beam narrowed. (Courtesy Brendan Finn)

Built in California and slammed on Randar wheels, Simon Hall's Mercury Barndoor caused a stir in the UK VW scene when it arrived in 2003: many didn't get it and many still don't. (Courtesy Simon Hall)

Jason Murphy of The Rust Box in California was another early Patina pioneer; his speciality was building slammed Patina buses with faded logos. (Courtesy Jason Murphy)

Discovered in a canyon in British Columbia, Canada, the Mercury Bus had been sitting since 1968; its first show outing was to the June 2000 OCTO show under the ownership of Rich Stewart, where Bus guru Charlie Hamill chose it as 'Coolest Barndoor.' (Courtesy Simon Hall)

beam, and a set of Porsche Fuchs wheels: according to Paul Knight, the archetypal Rat ride.

The popularity of Split Screen Buses was reaching fever pitch around 2002, with the UK in particular exploding in demand, often outstripping supply. The rate of VW Buses being imported into the UK from all over the world skyrocketed almost overnight. There had always been a few guys into early VW Buses and Patina, especially in the USA, but it was all fairly under the radar. George Schmidt, of The Butcher Shop in California, was one such early pioneer. As early as 1995, he made the first-ever narrowed front axle beam and fitted it to 'Money' Mike Hodgson's 1958 Bus. Other Californian guys, such as Jason Murphy of The

Rust Box in Visalia, soon followed; he built a heavily Patinated 1958 Bus, slammed to the floor, to the sides of which he added faded Speedwell logos. The Bus, like many other California VWs, ended up in Japan, and Jason built another, this time using an original paint 1963 Bus.

In 2003, the arrival of the 'Mercury Barndoor' to the UK, imported by Simon Hall from Devon, was another pivotal moment in the history of the Patina VW, especially in the UK. Here was a VW Split Screen Panel Bus, with faded Mercury Outboards logos on the front

Jim Buys' 1950 Split Beetle really put the cat amongst the pigeons at the 2003 Bad Camberg vintage show in Germany, when he showed up with lowered front suspension, early Porsche 16-inch steel wheels, and a healthy dose of Patina. (Courtesy Keith Seume)

doors, and, apart from that, pretty much 95 per cent surface rust across the whole vehicle. Added to the fact that it was slammed on a set of Randar wheels, which weren't available in the UK at the time, a lot of people lost their heads over it. I vividly remember seeing it pull into the Vanfest show in 2003 and feeling the buzz, as, love it or hate it, it was a huge rolling statement. For me, the Mercury Barndoor was a bit too Rat, and not the well cared for, sunbleached look that I usually like, but no one could ignore how cool it looked and how different it was from anything at European VW shows at the time.

Suddenly, Patina had become a buzzword in the VW scene. I remember going to the Bad Camberg show in Germany, in June 2003; the show is only held every four years and showcases the best early vintage VWs in Europe. These cars were traditionally Split and Oval rear window Beetles, which were generally fully restored, or well cared for original cars. In 2003 though, there was a heavily Patinated 1950 Split Beetle, owned by American serviceman Jim Buys.

Not only had Jim driven a car with rough bodywork into the world's most prestigious VW gathering, but he had also lowered the front suspension and fitted early Porsche wheels. Many of the purist vintage VW scene stalwarts didn't get it, up in arms that a rusty and modified car had been allowed into the show. Fortunately, Keith Seume did get it, and shot a feature of the car for *Ultra VW*.

Outside of Bad Camberg, and looking at the VW scene in general at the time, many other people refused to accept Patina too, thinking that owners of Patina cars were lazy or penniless (or even both). Falling into the latter category myself, I can remember how excited I was about building a nice-looking

John Jones' Barndoor 23-window 'Grandpa' fell off a cliff in 1967, whilst under Lin Ottinger's ownership. John was another early Patina pioneer; he painstakingly jacked out the heavily buckled roof and left the Patina as-is. The Bus eventually went to Spain, where it was fully restored. (Courtesy John Jones/Kustom Coach Werks)

car out of the rough 1964 Beetle which I'd bought as my first car back in 1991.

I'd taken the car off the road in 1993 to restore it, then realised that the body had been welded to the floorpan. Money being especially tight in those days, the car had sat in a garage for ten years until I could afford to restore it. The emergence of Patina cars and the Hoodride phenomenon though, made me re-think. While it looked rough, it was in pretty solid condition, and I began to imagine leaving the scruffy bodywork just as it was, fitting a narrowed front beam and a set of Randar wheels.

The crude Photoshop the author did on his tired old '64 Beetle, inspired by the Patina cars he'd seen on the internet back in 2004. (Author's collection)

Rusty Willey's '59 Single Cab was built by Kustom Coach Werks over ten years ago; he still uses it daily, in rotation with his original paint 13-window Bus. Rusty doesn't own a modern car and uses his Buses in all weather, year-round.
(Courtesy Rusty Willey)

The dry Colorado climate makes it possible to store Patina cars outside without much deterioration; Rusty Willey's truck is a Patina masterpiece, and just gets better with age.
(Author's collection)

The Hoodride explosion

In 2004, the Patina movement began to gather pace in a big way. I was an avid follower of the KCW website and forum, belonging to John Jones, of Kustom Coach Werks (www.kustomcoachwerks.com), in Grand Junction, Colorado. John and his team have consistently been turning out cool VWs for the last 20 years in a very timely (read: fast) manner. In the beginning, it was all about full body-off restorations and pastel colours, but around 2004, things began to change. KCW staff could be seen driving ratty cars with slammed suspension, which led to customers approaching John to build their Patina cars; these were cars that would be restored underneath, but still proudly wore their original paint on top.

The tide was turning as people began to realise that Patina cars looked cool; Patina and narrowed beams were another counterculture in the VW scene and were guaranteed to be admired at shows, mainly because they were so different to anything else at the time. The arrival of 'Dope Beat' Derrick Pacheco at Kustom Coach Werks in 2005, signalled a further change; it was Derrick who began a spinoff site while working for KCW – www.hoodride.com – championing Patina cars, and cool vintage and retro stuff. There appeared to be a huge proliferation of Patina cars being built all over the world, on the tightest of budgets, and overnight Hoodride exploded with popularity.

I was glued to the KCW and Hoodride forums, logging in each morning and several times throughout the day to watch the progress unfold on every car build. I followed the forums so much that I can still associate people's names with cars and vice versa. In contrast to the KCW site, many of the car builds on Hoodride were by guys with little or no skill. Some of the welding and metal repairs on these cars would have been comical were it not for their distinct lack of safety. What was more worrying than poor body repair on some cars though, was that some guys, despite lacking any welding skill, or even a decent MIG welder, were making their own narrowed front beams, following online tutorials from other car builders.

Safety takes a back seat

The distinct difference between cars built in the USA, where many states don't have any inspection laws, and Europe, where cars must generally pass a yearly inspection, became very apparent. Whereas many consider front shock absorbers to be important, for instance, lots of guys in the USA chose to run narrowed front beams without shock absorbers. Narrowing a front beam on a Beetle beyond two to three inches meant that the front shock towers needed to be modified, or built from scratch, and many guys decided that this wasn't necessary, or they couldn't be bothered.

This was always a contentious issue; there were forum arguments even in the USA, but when guys in the UK and Europe began to copy their USA brethren, many were very concerned about safety, especially when it came to the MoT rules in the UK. As time went on, despite some sticking to their guns and building shock-less front beams, thankfully, others began to think outside the box and fabricate shock towers for even the most narrow front beams. These would often be elaborately designed, out of laser cut and folded steel, to swing out from the end of the beam and clear the inner wing, while others would be short, tucking under the inner wing recess and running tiny front shocks from a Hot Rod or Mini.

Aside from the body repair and suspect suspension modifications, some went a step further, running spindle-mount front wheels designed for drag racing, making it impossible to fit front brakes. Others would make

An old KCW build from around 2009, Buddy's '58 Sand Green/Palm Green Bus was one of the first to run Randar RDW wheels. (Courtesy John Jones/ Kustom Coach Werks)

Franz Muhr's old L380 Turkis Patina Bug was driven daily, even in the harsh Colorado winters. The compound at Kustom Coach Werks, where Franz has worked for 18 years, is always home to some awesome Patina cars. (Courtesy Franz Muhr)

Franz Muhr's current daily driver; it's becoming rarer to see slammed cars at KCW these days, with most of the shop guys building stock height or raised VWs. (Author's collection)

Featuring an old red repaint, Franz wisely chose to leave his '63 alone and not attempt to strip it back to original paint. (Author's collection)

The original Hoodride stencil; Derrick Pacheco was a merchandising master and knew how to promote his brand. (Courtesy Derrick Pacheco)

the cars so low, that they would eventually scrape through parts of the car, including lower front beam torsion tubes. It seemed as though the scene was divided; some thought this kind of thing was stupid and dangerous, others saw it as cool and inspirational.

I'm sure that when Derrick conceived Hoodride, these unsafe modifications weren't on his mind; he just wanted to create a movement involving cool slammed cars, built on a tight budget, and it seemed he had succeeded. An explosion of merchandise, stencils and other branding took off and the word spread like wildfire.

One of the reasons that Derrick was employed by John Jones in the beginning was that he was pretty skilled when it came to online marketing. As well as making a success of Hoodride while at KCW, Derrick also had ideas about pushing the KCW brand; one of these was turning the KCW forum and website into a paid site. Although I'm sure a fair few people, including myself, signed up for the first month at least, it soon became clear that the website wasn't what it had been.

Then one morning, a literal overnight change saw the paid site being abandoned, and Derrick leaving KCW, moving to Arizona, and taking his Hoodride

For all those who disliked the Hoodride website based on hearsay, there were undoubtedly some awesome Patina cars on the site, like this original paint Turkis California Bug with an eight-inch narrowed front beam. (Courtesy Hoodride)

The author's '65 Beetle made an appearance on the Hoodride site once. It was a rust-free, original paint car, bought from Ernst Bernsteiner in Vienna. This picture is of the car when purchased; the black checks were stick-on vinyl and hid nice original paint with very few repairs. (Author's collection)

brand with him. John made it clear that he wanted to continue KCW as he had first set out; a business founded upon "passion and drive" and "effort and sacrifice" – simple hard work by John and his team.

By this point, Hoodride merchandise was everywhere, and Derrick seemed to have the world at his feet. He was promoting his website, brand, and apparent bohemian lifestyle, and the VW world was taking notice, fast. It was as if he were a celebrity and, all of a sudden, in 2006, he was being flown across the pond to the UK by Brian Burrows and Brett Hawksbee to attend the VW Action show and judge the 'European Hoodrides.'

By all accounts, the Hoodride part of the show was an amazing success; a large Belgian contingent drove over, spearheaded by Gianni from the Radikalbugz club. Many of the show visitors that weekend were amazed at how low some of the Belgian cars were, especially as many were not on air ride and had driven along the notoriously bad Belgian roads and onto a car ferry to get there.

Hoodride not all bad

As with the previous UK rise in Rat Look popularity, many interpreted Hoodride in different ways. My own rust-free 1965 Beetle with very nice original paint was featured on the site at one point (I'd moved on from the crusty 1964 car), directly below a 1953 Split Window Beetle with the whole sill and heater channel hanging off and the rear air vents crudely chopped out. Although many began to decry Hoodride for promoting unsafe cars, the site became more and more popular.

As bad as some cars were on the Hoodride website, there were also a lot of cars that featured nice original paint, were rust-free, and had a more sensible suspension build. The words Hoodride, Patina, and original paint seemed to be interchangeable. Much in the same way the words Rat and Rat Look were a blanket term for Patina cars three years before, Hoodride now seemed to be a catchall word for any car with Patina, but this was about to change yet again.

It soon became clear that all was not well in the Hoodride camp. Within a matter of days, a murmur of

VW forum gossip turned into a hate campaign, and, as fast as Hoodride had sprung onto the VW scene, it, the website, and its founder had disappeared, apparently with some merchandise orders outstanding. Hoodride, once the popular term for a Patina VW, was now a dirty word. Was this the end of the Patina craze?

Fortunately, it was not; it was just the end of the beginning. Patina car build forum threads no longer had a spiritual home, at least for a while, but the forum build threads featuring Patina cars just kept on coming, albeit spread across many different internet sites such as thesamba.com, restowagenuk.com and the now defunct lowlifevw.com. Many other forums also came and went.

The sad part of the way the internet evolves is that many websites are transient and often disappear when the server crashes, the hosting comes up for renewal, or the site owner moves on to pastures new. Thousands of car build threads and gallery pictures have been lost in this way over the years; more recently, the KCW site suffered a crash, leading to many of the early Patina

The author's '65 Beetle after being cleaned up and lowered. The 3-inch narrowed front beam was built at welding class, the first narrowed beam built by the author in 2003. (Author's collection)

Typical of sanded down fake Patina, Derrick Pacheco's Split Beetle was one of the cars he built while building the Hoodride brand. The car sparked controversy when featured in *VolksWorld* magazine, with one heater channel pictured hanging off the car. (Courtesy Derrick Pacheco)

The first full Patina build in Sweden, Martin Henrikson's car was given a full body-off rebuild while keeping the Patina paint. The car was later owned by the Belgian Radikalbugz crew, before being lost in a garage fire. (Courtesy Martin Henrikson)

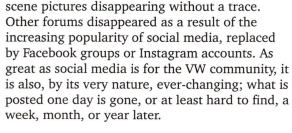

Right and Below: Built back in 2002, Patrick Hall's Wolfsburg-produced pressed bumper Single Cab was ahead of its time, and is still owned by Patrick today. It has a different Patina fade on each side, due to being parked outside for decades before he found it. (Both courtesy Patrick Hall)

scene pictures disappearing without a trace. Other forums disappeared as a result of the increasing popularity of social media, replaced by Facebook groups or Instagram accounts. As great as social media is for the VW community, it is also, by its very nature, ever-changing; what is posted one day is gone, or at least hard to find, a week, month, or year later.

Patina in popular culture

While many thought Patina was a passing fad, the same way '80s Cal Look was, it is definitely here to stay. Editor of *VolksWorld Camper & Bus* magazine (and former Editor of *VolksWorld* magazine), James Peene, has done much to bring Patina VWs into the limelight during his time at the helm. Patina cars are now very much a part of the magazines, with many Patina rides being regularly featured on the cover.

As well as car forums, social media, and magazines, Patina has become a buzzword elsewhere too; the word actually originated in the antiques industry, used to describe anything from the worn leather on an old chair, to the green verdigris covering anything made out of copper. More recently, while shows like *American Restoration* on Discovery have demonstrated how to restore original antique items to better than new condition, the success of TV shows such as *American Pickers* and *Salvage Hunters*, where guys travel around buying antiques to re-sell has brought Patina to the fore, and educated the

Another guy who owned Patina cars before they were cool, Ernst Bernsteiner's '65 Granada Red Fastback blew the author away the first time he visited in 2003. (Author's collection)

Opposite: The author's original paint 1968 Deluxe Microbus had very light patina and was featured in *Volksworld Camper & Bus* magazine in 2008. This was back in the days when a Bus like this could be bought for $2500. (Author's Collection)

James Peene, Editor of *VolksWorld Camper & Bus* magazine, has long championed Patina cars in print; this 1967 13-window Deluxe, built by the author in 2008, was featured by James. (Author's collection)

Built by Tony 'Skim' Wysinger in 2004, 'El Standito' showed a lot of guys the way forward; Skim has always excelled at cleaning up and polishing original paint cars and Buses, and has imparted his knowledge through several forums. (Courtesy Tony Wysinger)

Hajime from Japan drives his slammed Strato silver Oval Beetle through a tunnel at night. This is one of the author's all-time favourite cars, with a super-narrow front beam and rare accessory seat covers. (Courtesy Hajime)

Original dealer badges only serve to add interest and value to old Volkswagens; a European dealer badge on a car in the USA will always add an interesting aspect to its story. (Courtesy Tom Eitnier)

masses when it comes to owning something entirely original over something restored. People are beginning to realise that something, be it an antique piece of furniture or an old car, is only original once and, once it gets restored, that originality and Patina are gone forever.

As far as Patina Volkswagens go, both *American Pickers* and *Salvage Hunters* have helped to increase, if not the popularity, then at least the awareness of Patina VWs. Mike Wolfe, owner of Antique Archaeology (and star of *American Pickers*) owns several classic VWs and favours Patina cars, while star of *Salvage Hunters*, Drew Pritchard, also owns a 1952 Split Window Beetle with amazing original Patina. What better to

Original paint wheels and body parts are highly prized nowadays; note also the cross-ply tyres on this car, which always bestow a car with an original look. (Author's collection)

complement an incredible old enamel sign in the garage than an original paint car parked in front of it. It's often a shame when the popularity of something once cheap and accessible becomes expensive, and the Patina VW scene is no exception. In Sweden and the USA, what used to seem like an unlimited supply of dry, rust-free cars, with amazing sun-baked Patina, has gradually begun to dry up. Cars are still being discovered on a weekly or monthly basis, it's just that the value of original, unmolested cars, has now risen, often beyond that of fully restored and repainted cars. The world has finally noticed that a car is only ever original once and that this is to be highly prized in a scene full of cars that have had every trace of originality wiped out.

Where even five years ago most, if not all, Patina VWs were scraping the ground, with slammed suspension and aftermarket wheels, there has now been a definite shift, to preserving originality at all costs. Standard suspension, wheels and crossply tyres are now commonplace, with original paint wheels and

Andre Burchard lowered his first VW Bus after being inspired by Brendan Finn's '55 Kombi. He soon saw the error of his ways and has since built several stock height Volkswagens with a similar recipe. Cleaned up original paint and restored original logo buses are his speciality. (Courtesy Andre Burchard)

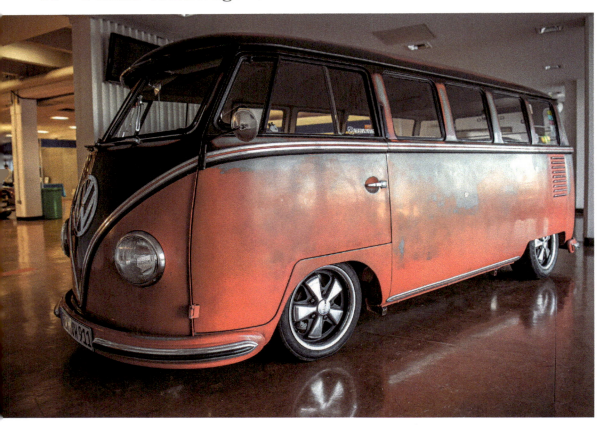

The guys at Reifenscheune in Germany debuted their Porsche 911-powered '57 Samba at the 2022 Volksworld Show. Although Porsche engines won't fit in a Beetle – contrary to popular folklore – they will fit in the back of a Split or Bay Window Bus. (Courtesy Martin 'Chuff' Wall)

body parts changing hands at a premium price. Old VWs are being treated like cherished antiques – who would have thought it.

Some guys get obsessed with finding not only nice original Patina cars, but also original parts, original paint body panels, and even original paint wheels; these often end up in private collections, never to see the light of day again, or end up receiving a light restoration/paint preservation, before hitting the sales market with a high price tag. If you've ever attempted to drive an old car for many years in a damp climate, you'll have experienced first-hand how parts like wheels deteriorate fast, and usually receive several coats of paint over the years. How refreshing, then, is it to see a car that not only has original paint on the body, but also on the wheels?!

Increased car values

Some may complain about the increase in value of original paint cars and parts; it has definitely put them out of reach for some. But when it comes to ensuring these cars are preserved, and will live to see future generations, the increase in value is actually a positive. No one is ever going to tool up and reproduce parts for a car that is practically worthless. If you've ever tried getting parts for an old car that is rare, or of low value, then you'll know what I'm talking about; at least with old VWs you can buy practically any repair panel, rubber seal or mechanical part that you'll need to keep it on the road.

Fortunately, the Patina obsession shows no sign of going away. People the world over now seem to genuinely appreciate the honesty of all things showing signs of age. The aforementioned TV shows, as well as Jerry Seinfeld's *Comedians in Cars Getting Coffee*, and shows like *Monster Garage*, and even *Wheeler Dealers*, have all done their bit for the popularity of Patina cars too. Even actor Ewan McGregor owns Patina VWs and is regularly pictured driving them in the press. The Patina VW scene really has come full circle.

CHAPTER THREE

From Rat to polished Patina

The differing styles & grades of Patina

There will always be, for most at least, some budget constraints when building a car. With the early and rust-free cars becoming rare and expensive, there is now a huge amount of creativity within the scene. For some, the word Patina, especially when paired with cars, will mean rust, sometimes even faked for maximum effect and attention. For others, the choice is an honest time-worn Patina on a car that is polished to perfection, with restored interior and chassis.

Each and every owner's unique representation of what constitutes a Patina car is what makes for such variety at car shows, and in magazines across the globe. There's nothing more tedious for some than walking down a line-up of perfectly restored cars at shows, so Patina is refreshing in that the character and flaws draw your attention and can hold it for hours. There's constantly something new to look at, and, for some, they find new ways to create the look, or transfer it to their own project.

As with any type and style of car, a Patina Volkswagen means different things to different people. When unrestored cars started appearing at shows, many of them were more Rat Look than Patina as we know it now. Even now though, no two Patina car builds are ever the same, and this is what makes Patina cars so interesting. In this chapter, we'll explore all the different styles, from Rat to Polished and even different ways of faking Patina – 'Fauxtina' – and we'll look at some of the methods people use when building these cars.

As you'll have ascertained from Chapter Two, the Patina car movement kind of happened by accident; back when it all began, unrestored cars were cheap to

The author actually got into an argument with his father when he decided not to paint this '65 Bus back in 2006. (Author's collection)

A diminishing supply of rust and accident-free classic VWs has led to projects being taken on which would once have been scrapped or cut up for parts. (Courtesy Pete Nickson)

buy as most people thought that they needed paint. I personally have lost count of the times that I would take a Patina car to a show, especially ten years ago, and have people ask when I was going to paint it. They then seemed put out when I said that I wouldn't be restoring or repainting the car. Some people would even become argumentative about it, including my own father. As time went on though, people began to get it. Once anything becomes popular, or 'trendy,' then the mainstream starts to follow suit and recognise the worth of certain things; Patina cars are no exception.

During the last 15 years though, whilst Patina VWs have become increasingly popular, the supply of genuine rust and accident-free original paint cars has begun to dry up – or the prices have increased to the point they are out of reach for many. Practically everyone who is a part of the Patina scene and regularly builds new project cars has had to adjust their expectations and start to buy some of the cars that haven't been so lucky when it comes to rust or accident damage. If you want to build a Patina car now and don't have a huge budget, then this is the compromise.

When it comes to my own projects, I've undoubtedly seen the above happen over the last 20 years; where once I wouldn't even buy a rare or early Split Screen Bus that needed rust repair or had cut rear wheel wells, I now take on Split Screen and Bay Window Buses that need both. It's a definite case of supply and demand which has not only pushed up prices but also made cars in much worse condition become desirable. I can assure you, if you had taken a trip around a VW junkyard ten years ago and deemed everything as total scrap, another walk around the same yard now would make you reconsider.

What this has done is bring more late model cars onto the scene, especially in the USA, where any model of VW younger than 1968 was once considered a 'Fat Chick' and disposable. What's more, people are generally more willing to take on serious rust repair and accident damage, whilst preserving and blending in the paint to match the original Patina. Whilst some still believe this is faking it, others think that it's completely acceptable. Sympathetically matching the original paint on repaired areas is a far cry from

The Type 34 Karmann Ghia – based on the VW Type 3 platform – didn't come out until 1961, but no one can deny the space-age influences in its styling. With lines that look like they came out of *The Jetsons*, Marcel Galima's car is right at home in Southern California, where much of the Googie architecture of the '50s and '60s still remains. (Courtesy Andrew Thompson/AThompsonsPhoto)

Although most people outside the VW scene only think of Beetles and Buses when they think of classic VWs, many models were available back in the day. Ben Lewis of Cornwall, UK-based Evil Bens chose a rare Australian Country Buggy – manufactured at the facility in Clayton, Australia – to put his stamp on. With plenty of modifications to make it this low, Ben chose to leave the ratty bodywork alone. (Courtesy Keith Seume)

building a Fauxtina car – where the car is completely repainted then sanded down to resemble wear or original Patina.

Of course, some people baulk at Fauxtina too, which is fair enough in the case of some cars, which are sanded down all over – in ways that the sun would never have burned-off the paint – then left to rust, effectively destroying a solid car. It's actually really difficult to match or create Patina, and make it look like original paint – much more difficult than simply repainting the whole car in some instances.

So, before we go any further, let's look at the different Patina looks you can achieve with any car – it's simply a matter of locating a suitable car and working out which look you want to achieve. Of course, sometimes the actual car you find dictates the finished look.

Barn Finds
Different to Rat Look cars (see below), 'Barn Finds' are vehicles that were usually stored inside for many years. Barn Finds may have been stored in dry or humid conditions, so there are a lot of variables when it comes to vehicle condition. The main aspect of Barn Finds is that they will have less visible Patina than cars that

Genuine original Patina, like this on Gibbs Connors' car, is very hard – some would say impossible – to replicate. (Courtesy Shin Watanabe)

were kept in fields or junkyards. They will have been shut out of the sun, so regardless of body condition, they have stronger original paint, or older repaints, than the hardcore Patina cars that have experienced the ravages of sitting outside in all weathers.

Gibbs Connors' incredible Split Window Beetle came from Sweden, and is typical of the Patina found on many Barn Find cars. (Courtesy Shin Watanabe)

Original logos on Buses are very sought after; Darren Franklin owns two such TV logo Buses. This one isn't original paint but has amazing Patina.
(Courtesy Darren Franklin)

Storing a vehicle out of the glare of the sun will usually help keep the rubber, plastic, and interior trim in tact, which will then usually be more pliable and may be able to be kept as is, or will only need small upholstery repairs, such as rotted stitching being replaced by a skilled upholsterer. Of course, many barns or outbuildings are home to rodent infestations, so Barn Finds may have interior problems caused by fabrics being chewed or made into rodent bedding.

Barn Finds will often be kept as they were found, so the Barn Find look may then evolve into Rat Look or polished Patina once the work commences to get them back to roadworthy condition. Barn Find cars are the ultimate for a lot of car enthusiasts; they represent a time capsule – a glimpse into the long-forgotten time when the car was stored away.

Although field finds and junkyard cars are great and often have more hardcore Patina, the thing about Barn Find vehicles that makes them the ultimate for many, is that they usually come with a known history, or it can at least be discovered. Finding the history of a car adds an extra element; being able to tell stories of a vehicle's past at shows, to your friends, or online, adds to the VW folklore, and makes any car that much more interesting.

Bobby Willcox is no stranger to building hardcore Rat Rides for himself and others through his company Milk and Two. His Oval Beetle wowed the crowds at the 2017 DTA show. (Courtesy Joss Ashley)

Rat Look

Rat Look was the term originally coined around 2002 by Paul Knight when writing for *VolksWorld*. It was originally a blanket term to include all Patina cars but has since evolved into its own specific look. Rat Look cars are generally built to look like they have just been discovered out of a junkyard or barn, and put straight back on the road, usually without even being cleaned.

Many Rat Look cars have dirty or cracked glass, rough, dented bodywork, and interiors that are field-fresh – they look like there might actually be a pack of rats living in them, and make many people want to get a tetanus booster or wear a particle mask before entering! Common features of Rat Look cars are dirt, stickers, rope-wrapped bumpers, and, in Europe and many other damp climates, a product like Ankor wax from Morris Oils applied to otherwise untreated surface rust. Many people also fit rusted accessories,

iron cross logos, plastic or painted-on rats, and other rusty roof rack art in order to make the biggest possible statement.

Let's look in more detail at all the elements that constitute a Rat Look car:

Firstly, a Rat Looker hasn't usually had any rust repair, bodywork or paint blending. This often means visible rust through areas, frilly, rusted body panel edges, and cracked or broken glass. Any added accessories or bolt-on extras need to have a similar look, or be artificially aged so they don't look out of place. Cars may have some of their mechanical aspects refurbished or recommissioned, or they may just be trailered to car shows without being made into running vehicles.

The key difference between Barn Find and Rat Look cars is that Rat Lookers are modified in some way. There isn't a distinct suspension and wheel protocol when it comes to Rat Look; many favour a nose-down Cal Look, or street racer look, whereas others fit slammed suspension so that the car is as close to the ground as possible. Some people will run Rat Look cars

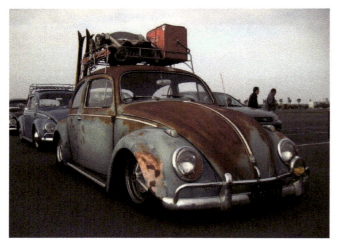

Spotted in the queue to enter the Bug-In 33 show in California back in 2008, this hardcore Patina car was sporting the Rat Look, with rough bodywork in some areas. (Author's collection)

with rusty original wheels or fit a set of original paint aftermarket wheels from the '50s or '60s with heavy Patina. There are others who will fit new chromed wheels to a Rat Look car as a stark contrast to the rusted bodywork.

Rat Look has always been contentious amongst VW enthusiasts, carrying connotations of laziness and lack of money. It was seen as somehow subversive, especially to purist types who felt that every car needed to be fully restored to be worthy of any attention.

Some in the VW scene still don't really get Rat Look. Personally, while I do understand the look, and feel drawn to heavily Patinated cars, I do take exception to cars which are devalued by scraping them along the ground or making them look worse than they are. Back when cars with heavy Patina were just considered junk, it's understandable that many of the Rat Look car builders would change the actual structure of the car to accommodate suspension modifications in order to get the car as low and radical looking as possible; they were just cheap cars out of a junkyard after all, and still in plentiful supply.

Fast forward 15 years though, and most of the

Very few cars have survived in the amazing original condition of Jason Reich's Gulf Blue '62. Jason has a knack of finding incredible survivor cars and giving them the full attention they deserve. He has plans to bring the paint back to a shine and fully detail the car throughout. (Courtesy Jason Reich/Air-Cooled Vintage Works)

Seen at the DTA meet in 2017, this '65 Beetle with awesome patina has a full air-ride install, enabling the owner to drive either standard height or slammed. (Courtesy Joss Ashley)

Andy Jewell found this all-original Yukon Yellow 1970 Beetle in Northern California and spent a couple of months cleaning and detailing it to perfection. The car has original chrome EMPI Sprintstar wheels and mild lowering. (Author's Collection)

While I have built and owned some very low cars, I have always had an issue with those that are built to scrape the ground, or had the floorpans hammered up to give extra clearance. Not only are cars built in this way dangerous to drive and a hazard to others, but these kind of modifications actively contribute to the destruction of a car, which has never seemed cool to myself and many others. Having driven really low cars and tried hard to avoid obstacles or potholes, I can honestly say that having part of your car bottom out is never a fun experience.

When the Rat Look came about, really radical suspension modifications were still in their infancy. Sure, cars have had lowered suspension since the mid-'60s in California, but tyre to wing/fender clearance was always an issue if you wanted to run really low, or to fit wheels which were wider or had a different offset to standard.

Narrowing the front axle beam didn't really become fashionable until around 2005, and even then, a lot of people didn't catch on for another five years, especially in Europe. When George Schmidt of The

junkyard cars are getting to be in short supply, at least those in restorable/buildable condition. What this means is that heavy modifications and excessive lowering of cars is much more frowned upon.

Lars Hardacker's slammed Split Bus wears the evidence of multiple repaints over the years and looks great slammed on white Rader wheels. (Courtesy Lars Hardacker)

Butcher Shop in California made the first narrowed beam on a Split Screen Bus, it was purely so the Bus could sit low and still have full use of the steering, without catching on anything.

From those early roots, a narrowed beam has become more about the tucked-in wheels look; for many, this has become a 'who can build the narrowest beam' contest, with beams narrowed up to ten inches becoming more common. As with the ground scraping, the narrowest beam contest can also be pretty dangerous; anything over three to four inches narrowed on a Beetle screws up the steering geometry and Ackerman angle, making the cars dangerous in a lot of instances without further modifications to correct it.

In the past few years, the lowest and narrowest contest has reached new heights; full air ride and hydraulic suspension systems, enabling the car owner to raise and lower the car at the flick of a switch, have become more common. Despite this, many still baulk at the use of air ride, and feel like being 'slammed static' (as in a static, not adjustable, drop) is a badge of honour.

This is fine, to a degree, but some of these cars are so close to the ground that they can't avoid causing a hazard to both their occupants and other road users; speed bumps, potholes and road debris cause a major problem for cars like this and it's not unheard of for them to break the suspension when getting jammed on manhole covers, and the like, at speed.

Sanded-down Fake Rat Look

If Rat Look has always been a contentious issue, then Fake Rat Look, or sanding down perfectly good paint to make a car look rusty, is an even bigger irritation for many. In my opinion, Rat Look cars are generally built to make a statement or get people talking, annoy the 'purists,' and to get attention wherever the car goes. Although this isn't always the case, builders of some Rat Look cars are often not too concerned with the welfare of the car, or its longevity – negative or positive, they're built to get noticed.

This attention-seeking seems even more prevalent with Fake Rat cars. It's unknown whether some owners actually think they are going to be accepted into the Patina crowd just by sanding their paint off, but whatever their reason for doing so, this form of 'customising' seems to be on the increase. Opinions do differ, but amongst the real Patina car crowd, creating fake rusty Patina on a car is rarely considered acceptable or cool, with only very few exceptions.

Cash-strapped car owners, or those just wanting to work with what they have, try to create their own Rat Lookers by sanding all, or much of, the paint off their cars, and applying substances to make it rust. This used to happen with classic Volkswagens but now seems to be more frequent on modern ones. Why people think that a rusty T4 or T5 Transporter, or a VW Golf or Polo looks cool beggars belief for many in the global car scene.

Ben Strong's late '50s Panel is rare in that it left the factory as a double door, ie cargo doors on both sides. It wears its original patina with pride, and needed few repairs. (Courtesy Martin 'Chuff' Wall)

The main problem with Fake Rat, whether it's leaving a hardcore Patina car to rust further, or sanding back paint to bare metal and making it rust, is that it ruins cars and shortens their lifespan. This is fine when it comes to modern cars – if you want to ruin and devalue a modern car, that's up to you, but when it comes to rare classic Volkswagens, many people are rightly saddened by this.

The classic VW scene used to be all about preservation and restoration of cars that are becoming rarer and more valuable as each year goes by. Sanded-down cars understandably cause upset, as there is no focus on either. Furthermore, when the builders of these cars become bored, or need a fresh dose of attention for being 'radical,' the cars are sold on, often to the first in a line of Patina wannabes who make the car look even worse and even more

Peter Nickson's Barndor Bus is a great example of a full-on Patina build: the Bus was once under a pile of cars in a Swedish junkyard, but has been repaired and sympathetically Patina paint blended. (Courtesy Peter Nickson)

Mike Heywood has a habit of turning out some killer patina builds; you can see the original L380 Turkis paint under an old green repaint that has mostly burned off his '63 Beetle. (Courtesy Joss Ashley)

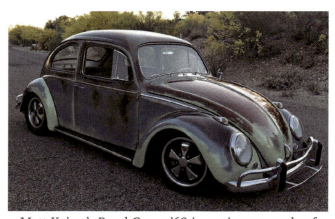

Matt Kaiser's Beryl Green '63 is a prime example of the kind of patina that occurs when a car sits outside for decades in the Southwestern USA. Mother Nature's finest patina. (Courtesy Matt Kaiser)

Dave Eadon's Kasan Red '72 Beetle was a huge inspiration for the build of the author's '68 Beetle. Not many people built post-'67 cars to this level until a few years ago, and being a UK car with patina makes Dave's car stand out. (Author's collection)

neglected – in many cases this is the same with all 'Rat' cars. Many of the nice, original, polished Patina cars that I have personally built in the last 15 years have ended up with an owner who confuses nice Patina with Rat Look and just lets the car go to ruin; I guess the only way to minimise the chances of this happening is to carefully vet prospective new owners.

Fauxtina repainted cars

There's a big difference between sanding down perfectly good paintwork on a car to make it look rusty, and trying to re-create Patina when repairing parts of an original paint car. Many don't see the point of repainting a car, then trying to distress it, but giving a car some 'dirty' Patina paintwork to match the original Patina is considered acceptable. As far as full 'Patina' repaints go, it takes about 20 per cent of the effort to paint a car like this, than it would take to bodywork and paint a car to show standard; many people wouldn't want to live with a show car anyway.

The problem with fully restored cars, is that you're always going to be worried about spoiling it. The beauty of Patina cars, on the other hand, is that you can use them as they were originally intended without being too worried or fearful of them getting damaged.

As original paint Patina cars have become more valuable though, a lot of people would be just as worried about leaving a car with nice original Patina unattended in a car park as they would with a restored car. At least a restored car can be easily repaired and repainted if it sustains damage; it can be nigh on impossible to recreate original paint and Patina.

So what's the solution? For some, the solution involves doing all the needed metal and rust repairs to a car, quick paint job on either a panel or the full car, then distressing it or giving it some Fauxtina. Doing paintwork or paint repairs in this way means that you don't need to worry about body working out any smaller dents, scratches or original Patina, as they will actually add to a finish that many will think is original anyway.

Quite often, the recipients of this kind of paint job, are cars on which the original paint really was too bad to be saved. As the original paint craze has widened, many people are now buying cars that were repainted years ago and attempting to strip the repaint off to reveal original paint (see Cars stripped back to original paint below).

There are a good number of cars that received little or no bodywork before having a cheap paint job 40 years ago, therefore there a lot of cars that have a lot of bodywork issues which only come to light when the paint is stripped off. These cars often end up having

The exterior of the author's old '62 Single Cab Pickup was mostly a poor old repaint, but that didn't stop it being wet sanded and buffed to a great shine. (Author's collection)

When Jason Reich started Aircooled Vintage Works, he decided to build a couple of patina cars as test beds for the wheel and suspension packages. His L87 Pearl white '63 has perfect patina, and the anthracite Cosmic wheels work well. (Courtesy Jason Reich/ Aircooled Vintage Works)

Fauxtina paint repairs, as the owners like the idea of original paint and Patina, and don't want to give up on the look and own a fully restored car.

The basic tips for getting a convincing Fauxtina job on a car are as follows:

1. Look at pictures of as many original paint cars of your type as possible and look at how original paint fades, before attempting to create Patina-look paint.

2. Match not only the paint colours but the original Volkswagen primer colours too – so many Fauxtina cars are let down by primer that is the wrong shade under the paint.

3. Apply paint very thin in the areas where you want to sand for Patina effect – don't just paint it thick, then attempt to sand off.

4. Once you've got your Patina areas, use a sponge or towel to add in some paint in small blotches – original paint has an orange peel look to it, so it fades in this way too.

5. Use very fine wet and dry paper to wet sand your Patina areas – don't take off too much paint too soon.

The final observation for those who still think

When the author saw this ex-Austrian 1968 Bay Window with original Porsche Gas Burner wheels and Porsche dealer door logos at Spa 2006, it inspired him to sell his '65 Split Bus and buy another '68 Bay Window Bus. The Porsche dealer concept has now been copied by all and sundry, but this Bus kept everyone guessing as to its originality. (Author's collection)

Jason Reich bucked a few trends by choosing a '72 Beetle as the basis for his 'Highwheeler' project. He searched for the very best original patina car he could find, so all the body needed was a buffing job on the original Texas Yellow paintwork. This car was built from the ground up with a fully detailed floorpan. (Courtesy Jason Reich/Aircooled Vintage Works)

Owen Eacott's UK RHD '67 Beetle sat in the family garage for years while he was growing up, after his Dad parked the car when it needed some work. The two fixed up the car for Owen to use when he passed his driving test. Believe it or not, this car has no air suspension; that's a static drop! (Courtesy Owen Eacott)

doing Fauxtina paint is pointless: how many restored cars have poor paint jobs because the painter was either incapable or too lazy to get the bodywork truly straight before painting? I know it makes me cringe a little when I see fresh shiny paint on poor prep work. The great thing about doing paintwork that's meant to look old is that there's no need to try too hard – once the paint is done (if you do a convincing Fauxtina job) then most people will think it's original.

Cars stripped back to original paint

Around ten years ago, when the popularity of original paint was reaching fever pitch on several VW forums, people began trying to strip older repaints from VW buses to try to find original paint. This has since become a style all of its own and is applied to vehicles across all VW models. Some would say that all cars are repainted for good reason, but the fact is, in the USA from the 1970s through to the 1990s, the abundance of cheap auto paint chains, such as Earl Scheib and Maaco, made it so affordable to repaint a car that many had cars repainted just to change the colour, touch-up small body damage, or to get more money when selling.

This situation wasn't helped by the '70s van craze, which saw a lot of Buses lose their rear wheelarches for large wheels and tyres to be fitted, and have paint jobs in fashionable colours of the era – think brown complete with orange and yellow stripes – to make them bang on trend. Luckily, these paint chains used different paint to the original VW 'Nitro Lacquer' and very rarely bothered to sand the car down. This means it's often pretty easy to strip these cars back to original paint.

Stripping cars back to original paint became more popular as the supply of good original paint cars dwindled, and was undoubtedly helped by a forum thread on thesamba.com, which involved people sharing techniques of stripping repainted areas without damaging the original paint below.

If you do decide to strip an old repaint off a car, there are certainly no guarantees as to what lies underneath. Some people choose to strip cars back to original paint and persevere, despite finding heavily damaged original paint, with lots of battle scars. Quite often, the paint removal method damages the paint below as progress is made, so proceed with care. Some people choose to remove the repaint and leave the original paint as it turns out, despite it essentially being a bit too far gone to look good on many cars. Others choose to blend the damaged areas in, or even end up

Michael Schramm discovered his original paint in the mid-2000s, when nice original paint buses with patina were inexpensive and plentiful. (Courtesy Michael Schramm)

The Stars and Stripes Bus is a regular attendee to the Mount Shasta Snow Trip – an event for Split Buses held in Northern California each winter. (Courtesy Mike Johnson)

Over 50 per cent of an old repaint has been burned-off this unique Karmann Ghia, revealing the beautiful original L41 Black paint underneath. Where some would choose to strip all of the remaining blue, the owner has made the decision to just polish the paint and run with it. (Author's collection)

going for a Fauxtina repaint, depending on how bad the paint is.

Depending on the preparation before the repaint and the type of paint used, there are several techniques that can be used to remove old repaints on these cars.

Perhaps the least invasive products used (and less likely to damage the original paint) are oven cleaner products, followed by select paint strippers (JASCO brand is often recommended on forums); experiment with several products and apply them first to a discreet area of paint for only a very time, building up the length of time as you progress and get comfortable.

Some types of paint are resistant to this and some people have resorted to both plastic and metal razor blades to laboriously scrape the paint off; this can take weeks or months, but the reward can be a very nice original paint car with minimal touch-up needed. On some Cellulose-based paints, it may even be possible to remove paint with lacquer thinners or brake cleaner. Whatever chemical you decide to use though,

remember to wear gloves and a breathing mask, along with some eye protection.

If all else fails, or you don't want to risk harming the original paint by using razor blades, you can choose to sand the repaint off the car. If there are numerous layers, it may be best to start with 120-180 grit paper on an electric or random orbit sander. Go carefully and stop to check the results often. If there is a single repaint or the paint is thinner, then begin by wet sanding with 800-1000 grit wet and dry. Use some salt-free dish soap in the water to help the paper glide and stop to wash off regularly; if you aren't getting much in the way of results, then switch to progressively coarser wet and dry – first 600, then 400, 320 or 240 grit.

Ultimately, it's up to you to decide what you want the finished car to look like; look on thesamba.com forums for inspiration and tips to get the finish you desire. Stripped repaint cars can end up looking like Rat Look cars, polished Patina, or even hardcore Patina.

Two-tone burned-off repaint cars

Some junkyard cars, that were repainted before sitting outside for decades, have had most of the repaint burned-off by the sun. This results in some pretty cool looking cars, often with very strong original paint showing through, as the repaint served to protect the original paint from the ravages of the sun. Whilst this is not original paint, it definitely still qualifies as Patina. Cars like this have usually had the repaint for longer than they were in original paint, and, while some decide to strip cars like this back to original

Although Chris Shelton eventually went on to restore his Baja Bug, it had a great look when initially purchased. A lack of popularity for a few decades means that there are still some decent Baja Bugs to be found, and many have great patina due to sitting outside for many years. (Courtesy Chris Shelton)

Opposite: Justin Heath's beautiful Notchback sports a half burned-off repaint, detailed Fuchs wheels, and packs a punch in the engine department; what a great way to get around. The bodywork was so rust and dent free that Justin just couldn't bring himself to touch it. (Courtesy Melanie Perron)

Jason Rider's all-original Oval Window Baja features the original Baja kit from Miller-Havens enterprises – the company that invented the kits in 1968. Jason's car has the original hood sticker, vinyl rear fender protectors and mahogany rocker strips, all with amazing patina. (Courtesy Jason Rider)

Steve Sanchez's Split Screen Single Cab Truck is the perfect example of a repainted car looking great as it is; it had the remains of old 'Oud's Hardware' logos under the yellow repaint, and was a great shop truck for Steve's skate shop. (Courtesy Steve Sanchez)

Originally imported to the UK by Rikki James, the 'Bob Saunders' TV Bus appears to be original VW Postal Yellow paint but is actually an old repaint over the original Dove Blue. (Courtesy Darren Franklin)

paint, many decide to buff up the paint on the car as it is and rock the two-tone Patina look.

Perhaps the best thing about having a two-tone repainted car, with original paint showing through, is that the result is truly unique. Volkswagen has used a wide array of original paint colours over the years, but the burned-off repaint cars showcase an entirely different palette of colours and make these cars truly stand out from the crowd at any car show or gathering.

Repainted cars with Patina

The love of original cars, and stripping back to original paint, is perfectly understandable; people have become obsessed with owning genuine, original vehicles. As supplies have dwindled, people have had to start thinking outside the box, and have begun stripping cars back to original before either running as is or blending in sympathetic paint repairs. There are times, however, where cars that were repainted a long time ago have just the right amount of Patina as they are. The cars that were repainted often when five, ten or 20 years old, and are now 50 plus years old, can have beautiful Patina on the repainted surface. In such cases, it's a bit of a crime to remove this paint in the quest of finding yet another original paint car in an original Volkswagen paint colour.

The fact is though, it is less fashionable to have a car with an old repaint, and the car will generally be less valuable with an old Patina repaint than if it were original paint. It's for this reason that a lot of these older repainted cars either get stripped back to original or fully restored and repainted. The shame of this is that these cars are

Darren Franklin has a bit of a thing for old logo buses; as well as the 'Bob Saunders' TV Bus and the Oremaster Bus, he owns another Bob's TV Bus, pictured here. Despite not being original paint, it would truly be a crime to strip this Bus back to original paint. (Courtesy Darren Franklin)

already beautiful as they are; even though they are not in original paint, they have a character all their own, and are survivors from a time long gone.

With the current trend of saving original paint or restoring, these older repainted cars with Patina are becoming an endangered species. The repainted car with Patina is kind of like the Heinz 57 mongrel vs the pedigree dog, but repainted Patina cars can look amazing if they are kept as they are and just cleaned and polished.

Hardcore Patina & clearcoated Patina

Not to be confused with Rat Look, hardcore Patina cars are those that have been out in the sun for a long time, often decades. What's left of the original paint may show in places, but a good 50 per cent (or more) of the paint will have been burned-off. Even in the world's driest climates, once the paint is burned-off or worn thin, any moisture in the air will eat through the porous paint and primer layers and cause rust to form on the surface. What many don't realise is that this rust layer can be cleaned off and will, in most cases, expose the original primer again.

Different car builders favour different looks: some may scrub off the rust staining on a hardcore

Here and page 74, top: Austin Cocks' hardcore Patina '65 Beetle was adopted from his late father, Chris', infamous Small Car Connection junkyard in Hesperia, California. The author recognised it on Instagram as a car he'd photographed in the junkyard many years ago. (Author's collection/ Austin Cocks)

Johnny Montana's original paint 1962 L390 Gulf Blue Beetle sat in an Arkansas junkyard for many years before he purchased it. The car is undergoing a clearcoated Patina makeover, with the underside being fully restored in the process. (Author's collection)

James Grigg's incredible L41 Black '62 Beetle has a unique story. It was bought new by a teenager in Georgia who went off to fight in Vietnam and never returned home. His parents decided to keep the car in the family and stored it for many years in their backyard, until they finally decided to let it go. James' friend Kyle Golding found the car. (Courtesy James Grigg/@getdealt)

James decided to take the body off the floorpan and do a full build on the car using New Old Stock (NOS) and new parts, although 90 per cent of the parts are original to the car, including the upholstery. The car features a 6in narrowed front beam with drop spindles, a raised fuel tank and 1in transmission raise. (Courtesy James Grigg/@getdealt)

Patina car, while others see this as sacrilege. Some think that hardcore Patina cars are the same as Rat Look, and in some cases hardcore Patina cars can be made into Rat Look cars. In other cases, though, they will be given the full treatment and turned into polished Patina cars, or clearcoated with mile-deep lacquer to seal it. Many see this as the best of both worlds – keeping the beautiful time-worn Patina on a car, and preserving it for years to come.

When it comes to building a hardcore Patina car these days, builders are faced with project cars that come out of a junkyard, and often have panels missing. In years gone by, especially on the original Hoodride forums, there were countless threads about how to make metal rust. Back then, it may have been to make Fake Rat cars, but nowadays things have moved

James is as into the water-cooled VAG scene as he is the air-cooled; this is reflected in the wheel choice for his Bug. They are one of two sets of South African Sprintstars/Rostyles converted to three-piece 17in by Mike Unland. Split-rim wheels are really popular in the water-cooled scene, and it's nice to see some crossover, especially when they look this good. (Courtesy James Grigg/@getdealt)

Despite the shiny patina look on James' car, it's all been achieved through polishing the original paint; he doesn't believe in clear-coating patina. You can see that one of the original rear light pods is L380 Turkis; this often happened due to factory quality control checks. Rejected parts would go back through the fitting and painting process on another car. (Courtesy James Grigg/@getdealt)

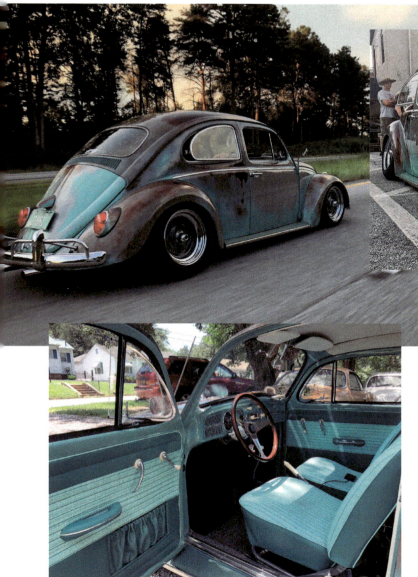

New on the South Carolina VW scene for 2018, Seth Wrobel's Turkis '63 Beetle has undergone a complete restoration, except the exterior paintwork, which has received five coats of clear lacquer. The car features full Jer-Fab air ride, with all airlift management hidden under the rear seat. Wheels are AP, restored by Chadd Magee, and measure 15 x 5in front and 15 x 17in rear. (Courtesy Seth Wrobel/401k Speed Shop)

on. There are times when you need to match the surface rust of a new panel to the car that it will be fitted to.

This can involve sealing the panel by painting it, then applying a special coating, often with iron filings or similar. Of course, if you live in a damp and humid climate, getting a panel to rust up to match the original Patina will happen a lot quicker, but there is usually a difference in colour when it comes to fresh rust (orange in colour) and older, more seasoned rust (dark brown in colour). This different appearance can, in some cases, be changed by applying different coatings to the surface.

When it comes to preserving a hardcore Patina finish on a car, there are several options available to

builders. Whilst the Rat Look crowd like to leave the car similar to a just-discovered Barn Find, complete with moss or dust-covered glass, cracked and hard-baked rubber seals, and burned-to-a-crisp interiors, many builders of hardcore Patina cars, especially these days, like to clean up and preserve the Patina.

The first step is a thorough jet wash inside, outside, and underneath, followed by scrubbing the Patina and paintwork with soap, water, and a household green scourer. If you're looking to tone down the surface rust, or at least remove extra rust staining, a product like CLR in the USA or Cillit Bang in the UK (limescale and rust removers) can remove rust staining with a judicious amount of scrubbing; the more elbow grease you put in, the less rust will be visible.

Clearcoating vs linseed oil vs wax

There has been an ongoing debate, for some years now, when it comes to putting clear lacquer, boiled linseed oil or wax polish over Patina. Some of the debate centres around the future of a car treated in these ways. Until recently, with advancing paint chemicals and techniques, clear lacquer applied

Jerry Lemieux'
clearcoated Patina car
was way ahead of its
time when he built it to
promote his
Jer-Fab shop many
years ago; the factory
black Ragtop car was
fully restored and
detailed inside and
underneath.
(Courtesy Erwin Stok)

directly over rusted metal only had a shelf life of a few years, before it would begin to crack and peel. Opponents to clearcoating would argue that applying it to a Patina car would eventually ruin the original Patina, as the lacquer would need to be removed at some point.

Likewise with boiled linseed oil; whilst it's a higher maintenance option and will require re-applying on a semi-regular basis, it's very difficult to completely remove should someone later decide to go in a different direction with the car.

The third option, which many in the polished Patina camp favour, is to apply several coats of a very high viscosity carnauba wax, such as wax meant for use in the marine industry. This will need several coats to be applied and further regular applications, especially in damp or salty climates, but will also be pretty difficult to fully eradicate if you make the decision to clearcoat a car later.

Ultimately, it is down to personal preference, but the choice must be made at the outset, as each method negates the use of another method later. The choice should also be based on the climate where the car is going to spend its life; if the car is going to sit out on the street in an area that is typically damp, or in the salty air by the sea, then wax polish alone won't protect the car unless washed and re-applied weekly. In these areas, clearcoat or boiled linseed oil may be a better option.

A car that is lovingly washed every time it is taken out, then stored in a dry garage, or one that is stored outdoors in a very dry climate, would be fine with wax polish alone, but as clearcoating and boiled linseed oil give the paint and Patina a darker and deeper lustre, many people in all climates favour these methods.

Clearcoating is seen as the ultimate compromise – owning a Patina car, and a shiny, well cared for car at the same time. It is also seen as a way to preserve the soul of a car, freezing the appearance so it never deteriorates.

Clearcoating tips

If choosing to use clear lacquer, attention will need to be paid to neutralising the rusting process and the acids involved before applying. Failure to do so will result in bubbling under the surface, and eventually the peeling of the lacquer. Various methods to neutralise the rusting have been discussed on internet forums and YouTube videos over the years. Everyone has an opinion, but through practice it has been found that the best results are achieved by scrubbing with soap and water to remove any loose or flaky rust, then using baking soda and water, or muriatic acid, to neutralise the rust, then washing again prior to applying the clear lacquer. This will give better results than simply applying it over untreated rust.

Early '60s project Bugs with great Patina and relatively little body damage, like Nate Jones' car, are getting harder to find. (Courtesy Nate Jones)

Nate Jones' beautiful Gulf Blue Patina car was discovered in the infamous Tom Tom's Volkswagen 'Museum' junkyard in Moab, Utah. The car is restored inside and underneath, using boiled linseed oil (BLO) to protect the Patina. The author was lucky enough to catch up with Nate and take some pictures of the car at Tom Tom's in 2018. (Courtesy Nate Jones/author)

Problems with cracking also occur because of improper application of the lacquer: as most people want to get the 'soaking wet' look, they apply the lacquer in one or two very heavy coats. This will look amazing upon application and initial drying, leading to the term 'burying it in clear,' but will likely eventually crack. The problem is, when applying thick coats, the surface will dry long before what is underneath. When the layers underneath eventually do fully cure, sometimes weeks later, they will have shrunk, leaving the hard, outer layer unsupported, causing it to crack.

Boiled linseed oil tips

Boiled linseed oil (BLO) isn't actually boiled. It is a chemically altered linseed oil, which dries much quicker than regular linseed oil, and is considered more suitable for applying over Patina, as it actually dries fairly quickly. When applying BLO, wash the rusted metal with soapy water and allow to dry. BLO can then be wiped onto the panel, and any excess later removed with a different cloth. It should then be left for one to three days to fully dry before the car is driven. While BLO will dry out and need semi-regular re-application, it will give a nice satin finish to the surface. Be warned, though: some dirt will stick to the surface and it can turn yellow over time.

The main problem with BLO is its volatility. BLO can literally combust on its own when exposed to air. The thin layer applied to the metal, when wiped off and allowed to dry, will be fine, but storing the product and, more importantly, the rags, can be tricky. Any rags used should be hung out to fully dry, before being sealed in a plastic bag and disposed of in regular waste. The main problems with combustion seem to be when rags are screwed up and left exposed to air, when they can literally cause an explosion and/or devastating fire.

Waxing tips

When it comes to the easiest method of preserving Patina, here are some tips for best results:

Firstly, wash and scrub the surface thoroughly with soapy water. If your sole aim is to maintain the appearance of an old Patina paint finish, you can then just apply the wax to preserve the look and rusty finish. Use plenty of wax upon application and follow the manufacturer's guidelines with regard to how long

For many, a 23 Window Deluxe – aka Samba – is the holy grail of VW ownership, and examples with original paint usually command higher prices these days than restored ones. After many years in the UK, Fabrizio Francavilla's Bus, with incredible patina, now resides in Italy. (Courtesy Riccardo Tosi)

Sean Pellegrini's incredibly original Beryl Green '63 is a true Survivor car; the original paint was polished and the car was mechanically overhauled. (Courtesy Sean Pellegrini)

Mike Heywood is one of the next breed of younger VW owners who isn't afraid of resurrecting original paint cars that have had a hard life. He builds superb scale models of people's VWs as a sideline, and does some expert patina blending, too. His all-original 1970 Bay Window Deluxe Microbus only needed mechanical work and some paint polishing to make it look like it does today. (Courtesy Mike Heywood)

Cody Goss' beautiful '61 Beetle 'Mabel' is progressively losing its original L456 Ruby Red paint each time he polishes it. (Courtesy Cody Goss)

Old stickers, such as this parking permit, are highly prized by Patina car owners; it's all about preserving the history on these cars.
(Courtesy Cody Goss)

to wait before buffing off the wax with a different cloth. There are various products available, from Rat Wax in the USA, to products like Collinite in the UK, which get rid of the chalkiness of an old paint finish and seal it, bringing out the natural warmth and colour of the Patina.

Whatever wax you decide to use, be aware that the more wax coats there are over the Patina, the better job the wax will do at halting deterioration and, if you require it, giving the car a lustre and shine.

Polished Patina

Polished Patina cars take a lot of work to build, often more than a fully restored car. Given that many Patina cars come out of junkyards, these cars sometimes have lots of parts, and even body panels, missing. Imagine putting together a jigsaw without some of the main pieces and you'll understand what it can take to build a sympathetically restored Patina car. On top of the actual restoration challenges that these cars pose, original paint body panels and parts now change hands for large sums of money; vendors of these parts know that there's someone out there who will swap an arm and a leg for that one missing puzzle piece.

If you can't find an original paint panel, the only option is to try and recreate the look on another panel. This involves not only matching faded original paint, which can be hard in itself, but also matching the

different layers of factory primer colours on the car. Polished Patina cars usually have the surface rust removed or toned down. With rusted cars, most is just staining; remove that and you'll usually find primer or original paint remaining, which can then be machine polished to a high gloss.

Polished Patina cars usually have nice original or full-custom interiors – the inside and underneath of these cars are usually fully restored, but the bodywork is cleaned up original paint. For all intents and purposes, these are restored cars, but with a clear focus on preserving the original paint; owners of these cars really know how to do the car justice and preserve the history of a car that is already decades old.

When it comes to VW Buses, they may even be rotisserie restored and fully painted underneath; many owners choose to faithfully recreate the factory overspray under the wheelarches, rather than painting in full gloss. VW floorpan cars, on the other hand, are often given a full body-off restoration, where they have a fully repainted and detailed floorpan. Usually they are repainted in the original factory colour on the undersides of the bodyshell, but have cleaned up and polished original paint on the upper surfaces of the body.

If you are looking to get a polished Patina finish, you will need to remove the old, dead top layers of paint. If the paint is really dead, then wet sanding with 1000-2000 grit wet and dry paper, using soapy water to allow the paper to glide better, will remove the dead layers. On rusted areas, you can scrub with limescale remover and a green household scourer to tone down the rusting and remove any staining. Following this, use some liquid cutting compound, either by hand or with the added help of a buffing machine, to bring a shine back to the remaining paint. You would be surprised how many cars – that many assume to be in need of a total repaint – will shine up like new with this method.

With the paint cleaned up and buffed to perfection, all that remains is to apply wax as per the manufacturer's instructions. If you do decide to clearcoat the car with lacquer instead of waxing, you will need to leave the car in the wet sanded (pre-buffing) stage, in order for the surface to be keyed enough to make the lacquer adhere to the surface.

Ryne Sanders' Diamond Grey '59 Beetle has strong original paint – not that you would have known it before he painstakingly stripped it back over around 150 hours, using acetone and steel wool. He also sourced original paint wheels when the originals were too far gone, as well as finding an era-correct engine to replace the absent original unit. (Courtesy Ryne Sanders)

Strong original paint cars

Some original paint cars may not even look like Patina cars at all; there are countless original paint Volkswagens out there that were well looked after, stored indoors, or out of direct, hot, sunlight for years, and have virtually no visible fading, surface rust or Patina. These 'unicorn' cars come along from time to time, even today; others are cherished, and form part of private collections. Many of these cars are assumed to be restored or repainted, and can be just cleaned, recommissioned in some cases, and used as they are.

The great thing about them is that they don't look like they need restoration to the masses. The downside, for lovers of Patina, is that the Patina is barely visible. Some even try to wet sand and buff these cars excessively to bring out more visible Patina. The problem, though, is that once the original paint is gone, there's no going back; it's only original once.

Deciding on a look

As with anything in life, every distinct look when it comes to Patina Volkswagens has its unique followers. Some people only ever build rat cars, or clearcoated ones, whereas others have built many different styles over the years. As I mentioned earlier in this chapter, many people feel that the car makes the decision for them: if you find a hardcore desert Patina car, then it needs to be built as a hardcore or clearcoated car. If you find one with less surface rust, then it may be a better candidate for polished Patina. Although many will have their opinions on how you should build your car, ultimately it is yours to do with what you choose. Take a look at the pictures, and decide what's right for you and your car.

CHAPTER FOUR

Slammin' formula

Building a lowered Patina Volkswagen

I n Chapter Three we explored the many different manifestations of Patina when it comes to Volkswagens; it really is a case of looking at what else has been built by others and using that inspiration to form the basis for your own car. As we have also seen, there are many out there who prefer their Patina Volkswagens completely standard when it comes to running gear and suspension height. Whilst the stock height Patina movement is gaining momentum, there are just as many others that feel that, in order to build a 'sick' Patina car, it has to have all the right bits when it comes to stance and wheels.

Built to be a solid driver that looked good but functioned perfectly, the author took a lot of time to get the suspension and steering right on his old '68 Sunroof. (Author's collection)

With a four-inch narrowed beam, drop spindles, and a modified steering arm, this original paint Bug had the right look, and handled and steered better than a stock Beetle. (Author's collection)

Having built a lot of slammed Volkswagens through The Bus Station (2002-2013), I figured out a long time ago what works when it comes to having a cool looking, but perfectly useable, static slammed Patina Volkswagen. Whether it's a Bug, Bus, Karmann Ghia or Type 3 you're looking to build, here is the Patina Volkswagens recipe – the path to getting suspension modifications spot on so you're not breaking things as you drive.

Before we go any further, it should be established that modifying anything has its drawbacks; if you modify one thing, then usually several other things will also need to be modified, in order to make things work correctly. The problem with a lot of slammed Volkswagens out there – especially in countries where there are no annual inspection laws – is that often the bare minimum is done, to make a car look slammed but on the tightest of budgets.

This is perhaps the reason why many still associate the word 'Hoodride' with dangerous cars; in the early days it was more common for people to follow this model, where the bare minimum would be done to slam cars and thus they would drive horribly, wear tyres out dangerously quickly, and not even be able to make a tight turn in the road. The 'recipe' below may not be for everyone, but it contains the experience that the author has gained from many years of modifying Volkswagen suspension day in, day out.

Disclaimer: When it comes to modifying any car suspension, please take advice from various sources and don't try to do it yourself if you don't have the capabilities. Modifying the suspension on a car isn't a good place to learn mechanics or welding, and it isn't a good place to make – possibly life-threatening – mistakes. When planning and buying suspension products for your car, please also consider the road traffic laws in your country. Some countries won't allow steering or suspension parts that have been welded for example, even if that welding is on a forged steel part and is carried out to a high standard.

Type 1 – Bug & Karmann Ghia

While there are hundreds of possible suspension configurations to take into consideration when building a slammed Bug, many of them only ever make a car look good; the aim should be to make a Bug look good *and* drive well. It's all well and good running a seriously narrowed front axle beam, but what does that translate to when you try and steer the car around a tight corner? Similarly, when it comes to the rear suspension; it's one thing to lower a car six inches at the rear, but how does that compute with tyre and gearbox wear?

It takes a lot of work to lower a Bus correctly, and the lower you go, the more work you'll need to do on every component; Jerry Lemieux's 'Burnt Westy' shows the very neat wheel tubs he had to fabricate for tyre clearance, complete with modified seat base. (Courtesy Shin Watanabe)

Limebug offers scratch-built four-inch narrowed front beams, as well as dropped springplates and air ride kits. (Author's collection)

When it comes to working out the stance of your Bug and how to achieve it, you will first need to make a wheel choice; a front beam that might work perfectly well with 4.5 x 15in Fuchs wheels, for example, won't work too well if you then change your mind and decide to fit 7 x 17in BRM style wheels or even 15in Randars with a completely different offset. Figuring out the ET figure of the wheel you are planning to use first will save a lot of headaches later after you've spent a lot of money and time, only to find that the tyres rub or the turning circle is hopeless.

When it comes to the Karmann Ghia, there's a bit more width up front to play with, so you may want to carry out some measurements (or search the forums at thesamba.com to see what others have done) and go with a slightly less narrow beam than if you had a Bug.

Front suspension

Using Fuchs style wheels as an example (the same would work for Cosmics or Gas Burner style wheels), a four-inch narrowed front beam, something you can buy off-the-shelf, is really the best possible compromise for a narrow look and decent turning circle when combined with drop spindles. Let's just say here: fitting a narrowed beam without drop spindles and trying to go low just won't work, as when you try to go low by using lowering adjusters alone, the wheel and tyre will sit way too far forwards; the trailing arms of the front axle beam work in an arc, so going lower on adjusters also means the wheel is moving further and further forwards.

Fitting drop spindles – although they do increase the front track width by $5/8$in, or around 9mm, per side – gives you an immediate 2.5in drop on a Type 1 beam,

without negatively affecting either the ride quality or steering geometry. Once you have your narrowed beam and drop spindles fitted, there are other options to take into account when it comes to setting up the car to drive well and go down the road OK.

The first thing you should always fit when lowering the front suspension of a Type 1 car is castor shims. These fit between the lower beam tube and the frame head of the car, pushing the lower beam tube further out than the upper beam tube. Castor shims were designed to restore stability when the front of the car was lower than the back of the car, but are good to aid stability on all lowered Type 1 cars.

It should go without saying that the tracking or alignment will need to be checked by a competent garage. You will, however, need to set it up somewhere close before you drive the car anywhere. Before you check the track width, you'll need to make sure that the steering box is centred – if you skip this step, you will be left with a car that wanders all over the road.

For cars with front suspension narrowed more than two to three inches, you will need to do some kind of correction of the Ackerman angle. As you narrow the front suspension beyond this threshold, the angle of the tie rods changes. This is not such a problem with the long tie rod, but it can become a major

Brett Elsmore's Karmann Ghia features an eight-inch narrowed beam; Brett alternates between 15in Cosmic wheels and 17in BRMs. (Courtesy Brett Elsmore)

The author extended the short tie rod lug on the steering arm of his old '68 Beetle to correct Ackerman and restore steering geometry – he got the idea from Russell Ludwig at Old Speed in Paramount, California.

Two companies now offer new extended steering arms: Limebug in the UK and Fresh Kustoms in Australia. (Courtesy Limebug/Fresh Kustoms)

problem with the short tie rod; this will begin to push backwards, rather than outwards, making the outer front wheel unable to turn enough on corners.

Correcting this issue can be difficult and there are usually compromises with whatever method you choose. Fitting a quick steer kit will help, but as it removes one whole turn from the steering lock, it can make the car feel more skittish. Some people have another tapered hole made in the pitman arm of the spindle, but the method I've found the most success with is extending the area of the steering box drop arm where the short tie rod goes.

For the rough alignment, I use a large and small steel rule to get the tracking somewhere near, by measuring against the wheel rim at a point towards the rear of the wheel, then a point as close toward the front of the car as possible. The front measurement should be one to five millimetres less than the back, so the alignment is slightly toe-in. The weight of the car must be on the wheels for this, suspension compressed.

Ball joint cars (1966 onwards) have the beam tubes spaced wider apart, meaning the frame head also sits lower at the front of the floorpan; going really low on

these cars is harder. You can trim off the excess metal that sits below the weld on the front of the frame head, as well as trimming and re-ending the lower adjuster bolt to give extra ground clearance. When attaching the spindle to the beam on ball joint cars, you should always set the camber with the concentric camber adjusting nut on the upper ball joint; the notch in the nut should face forwards when the wheel faces forwards for initial setup – the alignment shop will adjust from there.

When it comes to narrowed front beams, try to buy a beam with high-quality bushes or bearings, as many of the urethane type bushes wear quickly, causing problems with ride quality and safety. With some ingenuity, even beams narrowed five to six inches can be fitted with shock towers. There's an age-old debate going on, especially in the USA, about the use of narrowed beams without shock towers; some argue that the resultant increase in springing rate from narrowing the torsion bars inside the beam negates the use of shock absorbers/dampers.

Diego Vasquez' clearcoated hardcore Patina car was actually discovered by Jerry Lemieux while running his Jer-Fab shop in Southern California. The car features a narrowed front beam and 17-inch Rader wheels; it's fully restored underneath. (Courtesy Bait Media)

Another product worth considering if you're planning to go with a narrowed beam and drop spindles; Chase Hill produces extended trailing arms. These make the front wheel sit back further in the wheelarch, centering the wheel for aesthetics purposes, and making the tyre less prone to hitting the headlight bucket. Chase manufactures the upper trailing arm in a way that increases shock absorber clearance, too. (Courtesy Chase Hill)

While there may be some that have set up a beam like this and are satisfied with it, the use of shock absorbers is necessary to damp the springing action of the suspension. Countries with inspection laws will all require shocks to be fitted, and even in those areas without inspection, shock absorbers make sound sense from an engineering point of view. The best advice is to run oil-filled shocks at the front of the car, due to the excessive choppiness of gas shocks when it comes to ride quality.

Rear Suspension

When it comes to the rear suspension, it is possible to lower it by turning the spring plates on the rear torsion bars – one outer spline gives approximately two inches of adjustment, whereas one inner spline gives around 2.5 inches. By using the inner and outer splines, it is possible to raise or lower a car by any precise amount. Buy a magnetic angle finder or inclinometer for this job and you can work it out easier; four degrees of adjustment equals one inch in height change.

If you lower the suspension using this method, it will be best to fit gas shocks on the rear; turning the spring plates on the splines results in a loss of preload in the rear torsion bars, making the rear suspension excessively soft. If you are lowering more than one inner spline (2.5 inches), you will also need to notch the spring plate adjacent to the stop along the upper

Anyone can drop the rear suspension on a Bug, but it takes a bit more work to make it drive well and not wear tyres unevenly; drop spring plates correct toe on cars as low as Jason Reich's old '58 Euro Ragtop. (Courtesy Jason Reich/Aircooled Vintage Works)

It takes more investment to drop a Split Screen correctly than any other model. Jason Reich spent the time and money on his old '55 Barndoor Single Cab; it was his daily driver for over a year. (Courtesy Jason Reich/Aircooled Vintage Works)

edge; do this in a gentle radiused curve, as spring steel is more brittle than normal steel and more prone to sudden failure.

Lowering the rear of the car using the above method works fine to a degree, but do be aware that the lower you go with this method, the more the rear suspension will toe in, making handling and tyre wear a serious issue. You'll also need gas shocks on the back if doing this method, due to loss of rear suspension preload.

Type 2 – Bus – Split Screen

Lowering a Split Screen Type 2 is far more complicated, with far more options than any of the other models. Years ago, people used to fit a Bay Window Bus front axle beam to Split Buses, especially in Europe; 1968-69 ball joint beams bolt right onto the Split Bus chassis rails, unlike later, 1970 onwards, ball joint beams. The main issues with fitting a ball joint beam to a Split Bus, if you're planning to go low, is that they sit one to two inches higher than a link pin Split Bus beam and the track width is 66mm wider: clearly no good if you're looking to narrow the front suspension, but great if you're looking to raise it.

Front suspension

When it comes to lowering the front of a Split Bus, the age-old recipe is to narrow the front beam by four inches and fit 'flipped' drop spindles. Just because this

is an age-old recipe, though, doesn't mean it's the right thing to do for you and your Bus. Although people like the uber-tucked look that a four-inch narrowed beam gives, going four inches narrowed with some wheels will give you more tyre clearance issues than if you went for a two-inch narrowed beam. Standard steel wheels and wheels with a tucked offset, like Porsche Fuchs style wheels, will sit in the sweet spot in the wheel well with a two-inch narrowed beam, whereas with a four-inch beam you will have to tub the arches to get the Bus to sit as low. Of course, if you plan to run wheels with a lower ET figure, like Randar wheels, BRM, or EMPI five-spoke types, then a four-inch narrowed beam may be better for you.

Flipped spindles seem to have become the industry standard in the last ten to 15 years, and it's easy to see why; they can be built by anyone with moderate skills,

A freshly-built set of 'flipped' Split Bus drop spindles; these have become the standard way to lower Split Buses and link pin beam equipped Bay Windows. (Author's collection)

A four-inch narrowed front beam has become the basic standard for lowering a Split Bus and giving it a radical look. This one is owned by Steven Kretschmar. (Author's collection)

The perfect answer to setting up the correct caster angle on a narrowed Bus beam; Dog Back Performance beams are manufactured with eccentric caster adjusters around the mounting bolt holes.
(Courtesy James Peene)

The author mid-way through narrowing a Split Bus lower trailing arm shock mount; this allows the shock absorber to sit vertically on four-inch narrowed beams.
(Author's collection)

The author raising the centre pin housing on a Bus beam for extra ground clearance; this also requires shortening and re-notching the pin.
(Author's collection)

and are not two spindles welded together, which seems to scare people even when carried out professionally. The main issues when it comes to 'flipped' spindles though, is that they mess up the castor angle and run only a single thrust surface, rather than the double thrust of stock height spindles. There's also the issue of the tie rods hitting the chassis with flipped spindles, as the pitman arm sits higher up the spindle in relation to stock; very low Buses with flipped spindles will need the chassis to be notched for clearance.

When it comes to welded drop spindles, especially ones from a reputable shop like Old Speed or Wagenswest, they run dual thrust faces like a standard spindle and don't mess up the castor angle. The pitman arm will also sit in the stock location with these spindles, so you won't need to notch the chassis. They really do make a lot of sense over flipped spindles, but the welding aspect scares most people off. So, what's the solution to correct the castor angle when running flipped spindles? A beam with castor correction built in.

When I ran The Bus Station Slammin' Shop (TBS),

we experimented a lot on Bus beams when it came to castor correction; with a Bus beam, it isn't a simple case of fitting castor shims, but the castor correction has to be built into the structure of the beam. At TBS, we settled on seven degrees of castor correction on TBS scratch-built Bus narrowed beams and it gave great stability at speed; I once took a one minute video of my '62 Single Cab going die-straight down the highway with both hands off the steering wheel. This is in stark comparison with off-the-shelf narrowed Bus beams used by most other companies at the time, which needed constant steering correction on the highway to keep the Bus in a straight line.

When it comes to buying a Bus beam with in-built castor correction these days, the guys at Dog Back

Performance, in Germany, seem to have the market cornered; their beams come with concentric castor adjustment nuts around the mounting bolts, much like the camber nuts on the upper ball joint of late model Volkswagens.

The other modification that needs to be made on a four-inch narrowed beam is to narrow the lower shock mount on the front trailing arms; this needs to be narrowed in order for the shock absorber to sit at the correct angle. If you choose not to do this, not only will the shock sit at an angle, putting strain on the rubber bushes, but it will also foul the beam mounting bolts on most beams.

The last modification that needs mentioning here when it comes to narrowed axle beams is the steering centre pin. On some off-the-shelf narrowed Bus beams and on stock beams, the Split Bus centre pin sits around an inch lower than the centre steering pin housing on the beam. If you want to reduce the chances of hitting anything in the road though, this really needs to be raised up flush to the bottom of the housing; the pin will also need to be shortened and re-notched, and the lower bush driven further in.

Steering box raise
Even when it comes to running a sensible height on a lowered and narrowed Bus, the steering box will be too low to the ground, so many people choose to raise it. Raising the steering box around 1.5in can be done without any modifications to the cab floor. There are laser cut and folded steering box raise kits available if you're not keen on cutting and welding the chassis

A laser cut steering box raised chassis section freshly welded into the author's old 1962 Single Cab; these parts enable the box to be raised by 42mm, but require a small bulge to be made in the cab floor for clearance. (Author's collection)

section where the steering box bolts up; the standard raise on these is 43mm, which does necessitate a slight bulge to be fabricated in the cab floor. These, along with a new clearance pedal arm are available through Hayburner – www.hayburner.co.uk.

If you don't want to 'hack' your Bus and raise the steering box, you could fit one of the available steering rack kits on the market. In my experience, the most popular brand tends to give the steering a very tight feel, though, and needs endless minor correction when driving. Like I said earlier, any modification you make will have a knock-on effect in other areas and sometimes compromises have to be made. If it were my choice, I would always keep the factory steering box.

Rear suspension
From the factory, Split Screen Buses came with reduction boxes at the ends of the rear axle tubes, effectively raising the ground clearance by 3.5in. Going any lower than a couple of inches at the rear on a Split Bus means getting rid of the reduction boxes – there are two basic methods of doing this, but there are a lot of options when it comes to the actual parts you can use and kits that are available.

One of the main reasons for getting rid of the reduction boxes when going low is that, as the oil supply to the reduction boxes needs to run down the axle tubes from the gearbox, lowering a Bus to the point that the axle tubes are at a higher angle means that this oil supply will be interrupted. Lowering more than a couple of inches will also result in excessive rear wheel camber, and will cause the bearings and gears to wear at a faster rate.

The third good reason to get rid of the reductions on lowered buses is the gearing; reduction boxes were employed by Volkswagen on the first generation Transporter as a way of making a fully-loaded 25hp Bus go up steep hills. As engine size and spec increased, this raised gearing was less necessary; most Split Buses these days are running at least double this original horsepower.

When it comes to getting rid of the reduction boxes, there are two main methods to use; Straight axle and independent rear suspension (IRS). Even though there are just two methods, there are several ways of carrying out the modifications, with a wealth of different kits and parts available for either method.

Straight axle
Generally accepted as the best method for going low, doing a straight axle conversion on your Bus will mean lowering the rear a minimum of 3.5-4in. Many

Straight axle conversions are the most popular method of getting a Split Bus to sit low; the author lowered Johnny Montana's late '63 Mouse Grey Westfalia in 2009 – it's an accomplished road-tripper. (Courtesy *VolksWorld Camper & Bus* magazine)

A fully refurbished late Beetle gearbox ready to fit into the author's old 1962 Single Cab Pickup. (Author's collection)

people use Bug gearboxes when using this method, but it is also possible to flip the differential in your standard gearbox (not flipping the diff will cause you to have four reverse gears and one forward gear).

Traditionally, straight axle kits would consist of modified spring plates and custom length axle tubes, running early short end castings with extended tubes. You would also need to source early bearing caps

and long axles. A few years ago, though, a couple of different people came up with the adaptor style kit. With this type of kit, you could simply bolt in a long or short axle gearbox, complete with original axles and tubes; the adaptor kit consists of spacers to space the mounting flanges for the axle tubes inboard of the spring plates.

There's a fair bit of snobbery around when it comes to original style or adaptor kit; I've used both when running The Bus Station and I found the adaptor kit perfectly adequate and reliable in the Buses I used it on; it also came in at a lower cost and required less work to fit. The adapter kits use either 1968-69 Bay Window spring plates or cut down and re-drilled Split Bus spring plates.

There is a third method to employ when straight axling a Split Bus; you can narrow the rear torsion housing and fit up any short or long axle gearbox complete. This method is much more invasive and harder to return a Bus back to stock if it is carried out, but it works well, especially if you plan to run much wider rear wheels; you can get the same outcome with an adaptor kit with short axles though, so cutting and narrowing the rear torsion housing isn't really necessary.

The Jiffy Panel Bus was lowered back in 2002 by Eric Carlson in Spokane, Washington. He used the recipe that has become standard for Split Buses: narrowed beam, drop spindles, and straight axle conversion. The Bus is now owned by Ed Skellett in the UK. (Courtesy Ed Skellett)

A radiused notch in the upper spring plate of a straight axle converted Split Bus to give extra clearance; a sharp corner here would make the spring steel prone to sudden failure. (Author's collection)

Independent rear suspension (IRS)

When it comes to most IRS kits, you can run at stock height or a mild suspension drop. IRS is also suitable for airbag suspension, but usually, the kits and the Bus need substantial modification for this to happen. When it comes to IRS kits, the main distinction to make is whether you want to use Bay Window Bus parts or Beetle IRS parts.

Bay Window based kits

There are a few different Bay Window based kits out there, which use modified Bay Window trailing arms and spring plates, as well as the Bay Window hubs and rear brakes. You can either go for bolt-on kits, which contain bolt-on torsion bar brackets, or weld-on kits. The bolt-on kits are generally better, as they allow you to set up the camber and alignment correctly before welding.

There are also kits where the entire rear frame horns are removed and replaced with new ones; these kits are well thought out when it comes to alignment, etc, but mean it is very difficult to put a Bus back to stock if ever this is required.

Beetle based kits

Beetle based kits require you to use the swing arms, hubs, and brakes from a Beetle, and are a little lighter than Bus based kits; they also offer better/less expensive brake options. This is especially so if you plan to run a custom bolt pattern, or change to Porsche bolt pattern. The Beetle based kits allow the use of late Bug brakes and hardware, larger Type 3 rear brakes, or even Porsche 944 rear disc brakes or aftermarket disc brakes.

With either method of IRS conversion on a Bus, adjustable spring plates or extended drop plates can be used. With the Bay Window based kits, you can also run horseshoe plates to gain extra drop, although certain aftermarket wheels won't fit with the horseshoe plates, as they widen the rear track width.

It's also possible to run stock height with IRS; if you're looking to keep a Split Bus stock height, but have the benefit of better gearing and handling and less noise while driving, then IRS makes a lot of sense. In order to run stock height with IRS though, you will need to run Type 181/182 'Thing' rear drive axles, flanges, and CV joints, as these have more travel.

Type 2 – Bus – Bay Window
Front suspension

As with the Split Screen Bus, there now seems to be a generally accepted way to lower a Bay Window Bus and still retain good ride quality. Until about ten years ago, most people lowering a Bay Window Bus would narrow the existing front beam. As Bay Window beams have needle roller bearings in the ends, they were always much harder to narrow correctly. With the bearings in the ends, the usual method to narrow

IRS conversions are good for stock height or a mild drop if you want to remove the original reduction boxes, as fitted to Bubba's '64 Turkis Camper, and have better highway gearing. (Author's collection)

a Bay beam was to make an offset cut in the centre of each beam tube and remove the required amount from the centre of the beam. In order to mount the narrower beam up to the chassis rails, the original shock towers would then need to be removed in their entirety, before new laser cut flat plates could be welded on.

As time went by and a few people began to convert to Split Bus/link pin beams up front, complete with flipped drop spindles, this became the accepted method of narrowing and lowering the front of a Bay Window. The pros of doing a conversion like this are many; the Split Bus beam lowers the front of a Bay Window Bus one to two inches over a Bay/ball joint beam. When you add on flipped spindles (3.5in drop), you are already around five inches lower than stock, without compromising much ride quality; it's true that ball joint beams ride a little softer, but to go five inches lower and only lose a little softness was unprecedented in years gone by.

Another one of the pros of using a Split Bus beam is that, even without narrowing the beam, the front track width is already 66mm narrower (around 2.5in). This means that much wider wheels or those with a bigger offset can be fitted when using a Split beam. Flipped drop spindles narrow the track width a further 9mm per side, so even a stock width Split Bus beam fitted to a Bay with flipped spindles is three inches narrower

than stock. Of course, many still choose to narrow a Split Bus beam when fitting to a Bay, to create the most radical look possible, but it isn't always the best method to employ in order to make everything fit well and work correctly.

There are quite a few Bay Window buses out there with four-inch narrowed Split beams fitted, that are also super-low and fitted with wheel tub extensions to accommodate the wheels and tyres at the required height. Many of these wouldn't need tubs if they had been narrowed a lesser amount and had the wheels sitting in the sweet spot inside the wheel well.

When it comes to fitting a Split beam to an early (1968/69) Bay Window, the front brake options are easy if you want to retain the wide five (5 x 205mm) bolt pattern. The only difference between 1964-67 and 1968-70 front brakes is that the grease seal in the later drum is a different diameter. If you want to convert to Porsche bolt pattern on the early Split Bus spindles, you can use many of the available kits to fit early Porsche 944 non-turbo front discs. There are also kits available using Wilwood and other four-pot calipers.

If you are looking to fit a Split Bus beam to a 1970 Bus, then the brakes will be the same as for 1968 and 1969, but where the beam bolts up to the chassis will be different. Luckily, the manufacturers of narrowed link pin beams and end plates these days tend to put

It takes a serious amount of work to get any Bus to sit as low as Andrew Cooke's Titian Red '68 Deluxe – notching and tubbing of the chassis and bodywork are just the beginning. (Courtesy Joss Ashley)

both sets of holes in the end plates, so they can be mounted onto the 1970-79 chassis rails.

When it comes to front brake options on the 1971-79 Bay Window buses, however, things are a little trickier. If you're looking to retain the original 5 x 112mm bolt pattern, you can buy Brazilian front spindles and have them made into flipped drop spindles; with the Brazilian spindles, you can run late 1973 onwards discs and calipers. Of course, you could retrofit drum brakes onto a later Bay Window Bus, but it really makes no sense to do so.

Rear suspension
When it comes to lowering the rear suspension of the Bay Window, many do so simply by turning the spring plates a notch or two on the inner or outer splines. This is fine to a degree, but if you lower more than one spline using this method, the toe-in of the rear suspension will be excessive. It's better to use extended drop spring plates: in this way you can drop a set amount and the toe will be corrected to factory spec, giving you better handling and less tyre wear.

17in wheels – as fitted to this Early Bay Westfalia with great patina – have become more fashionable in recent years, although it takes a lot more work to get any VW this low with 17s fitted. (Courtesy Niels Timmerman – *Airmighty* Magazine)

Adjustable spring plates allow the rear suspension to be fine-tuned, without dismantling it. Make sure you buy extended ones to correct rear toe.
(Author's collection)

When fitting horseshoe lowering plates, you can get away with a small notch for driveshaft clearance, such as on this '69 Deluxe Bus. (Author's collection)

Type 3s can be made to sit pretty low with the original front suspension; the limiting factor is usually how low the front beam and frame head hangs down. (Courtesy Cody Goss)

A variety of other products are available to lower the rear of a Bay Window, including adjustable spring plates, which are good for fine-tuning the ride height and horseshoe plates which bolt between the spring plate and hub, giving a three-inch drop. The only issue with horseshoe plates is that they increase the rear track width by around 10mm, which means fitting horseshoes with certain aftermarket wheels isn't possible.

When lowering the rear of a Bay Window more than four to five inches, it will be necessary to notch the chassis for driveshaft and/or swing arm clearance, depending on what method you have employed for the rear suspension modifications; if using horseshoe plates you can get away with a small notch for the driveshaft, but using other methods will necessitate a larger c-notch. There are now a few companies selling laser cut and welded frame notch kits, which make the job easier but do be aware that once done, it will be hard to return to stock.

Type 3 – Fastback, Squareback, Notchback, T34 Karmann Ghia

For the first time in the history of Volkswagen production, the Type 3 range had completely re-designed front suspension. It utilised solid torsion bars, rather than leaves, which crossed over inside the front axle beam. This meant that Type 3 models were equipped with better ride quality and handling.

While the accepted method for lowering and narrowing the front end of a Type 3 nowadays seems to be fitting a narrowed Type 1 beam assembly, this is actually a backwards move in terms of both ride quality and handling. The Type 1 beam conversions mainly came about because of the need or desire to narrow the front suspension and the realisation that it is very difficult to narrow the original Type 3 front beam, as the solid torsion bars cross over and are splined at the outer ends.

Lower front (original beam)

To lower the Type 3 models with stock suspension, it's a simple matter of adjusting the torsion bars on the splines both in front and at the rear; a Type 3 lowered by this method, as long as carried out correctly, has always meant that lowered Type 3s still retained good ride quality. The main bugbear when lowering a Type 3 and retaining the original front beam though, is that the lower frame horns, where the original beam attaches, hang down really low, causing clearance problems even on cars that are only moderately lowered.

Carl Taylor's amazing matching numbers Ruby Red Notchback was imported from Germany, where it spent much of its life. It's believed to have only driven 45,000km from new and has been sympathetically renovated, but the original bodywork was kept as-is, except for a full polish. It retains the factory Type 3 suspension, and is lowered by turning the torsion bars on the splines. (Courtesy Martin 'Chuff' Wall)

There are things that can be done to increase the ground clearance here, though; Ben Lewis of Evil Bens, Cornwall, came up with a modification to the beam mounting area, making the frame head of cars less likely to hit the ground. When it comes to narrowing the front suspension, Old Speed in Paramount, California, have designed and built narrowed Type 3 front trailing arms and drop spindles, which are jig built and welded to a very high standard.

There's something really radical about a narrowed Type 1 beam on a Type 3, especially when combined with the sleek lines of an early shape Fastback, such as Colin Pace's old car. (Author's collection)

Type 1 conversion beams

Of course, if you want to go really low, then Type 1 conversion beams are available from a variety of suppliers, allowing you to fit either a link pin or ball joint Type 1 beam, complete with drop spindles, to the front of your Type 3. When fitting a Type 1 beam, it is necessary to remove the lower frame head horns from the front of the floorpan if you want to increase ground clearance, but doing this makes it very hard to put a car back to stock in future.

Rear suspension

Lowering the rear of a Type 3 is very similar to lowering the rear of a Bug; Type 3s were swing axle up to 1968, then IRS from 1969 onwards. Type 3s

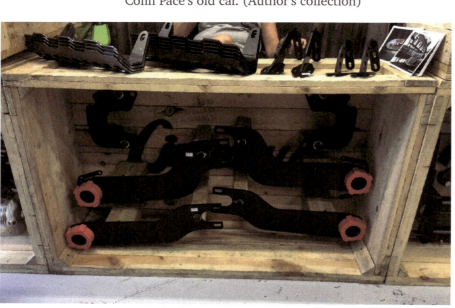

Adjustable spring plates can help with fine tuning suspension height, but if you are planning to lower more than two inches, you should really look to fit some extended drop spring plates. Available in several preset heights, the drop spring plates – such as these offered by Limebug – are the ideal solution for going low without ruining tyres regularly by scrubbing off the inner edge due to excessive toe in. (Author's collection)

Ben Lewis' Slammed '71 Westfalia took a lot of work to get this low, and it keeps evolving. He's recently narrowed and tubbed the rear suspension to accommodate wider rear wheels. Note the aged-looking signwriting he added to promote his company. (Courtesy Joss Ashley)

The author's 1962 Single Cab was proof that lowered Buses can drive great; the owner-designed beam end plates with seven degrees positive caster meant that it drove in a straight line and handled very well. (Author's collection)

can be lowered by adjusting the spring plates on the splines, but this will affect toe-in, so if lowering more than a couple of inches, it's best to fit extended drop spring plates to the rear – doing so will give better handling and less tyre wear.

Summary

This guide to carrying out suspension modifications to your Volkswagen isn't meant to be a how-to guide, just an overview as to what is available parts-wise, and an opportunity to impart a few tips learned from years of lowering air-cooled VWs. Please continue to be aware of safety when it comes to carrying out suspension and brake modifications, and realise that the lower you go, the more modifications to every moving part will be necessary in order for everything to function correctly.

Ultimately, what you do to your car is up to you, but do bear in mind the rarity of good cars now and future values when it comes to making modifications that will be hard or, in some cases impossible, to return to stock in the future. There are some people who think that heavy suspension modifications and hacks are like the

The author fabricating small tie rod chassis notches on his '62 Single Cab pickup; the use of flipped spindles makes this necessary when going low. (Author's collection)

cut rear wheelarches of this generation; lots of these cars will eventually be devalued because they can't be easily restored.

CHAPTER FIVE

The Patina economy

The people behind Patina Volkswagens

This chapter explores the multi-faceted community of the Patina Volkswagen owner and builder, and how rising car values and perceived value of original cars (over restored ones) have generated, not only a trendy new scene, but also an economy surrounding it. I also take a look at the recipe for producing a winning Patina car, and expand on some of the most popular modifications.

With a growing interest in Patina cars, and therefore rising values, Patina project cars, in particular nice original cars, are becoming out of reach for some.

There is a larger number of high-dollar cars being churned out by professional shops and several professional dealers in Europe, the USA, and as far afield as Japan, catering for wealthy clientele. If your day job doesn't afford you this luxury, there is another way. Like me, you'll need to rely on lucky purchases, and possessing the skills to restore the car to its full potential.

Rather than sit back and gripe about the price rises though, many in the Patina VW scene have adapted – and overcome them – by buying cars to flip until they can afford the one they want to keep for a while, or maybe forever. With a few exceptions (some just love one particular year or model of car), people generally start with later, more affordable models, trading up to earlier and earlier years. There has always been a tendency in the VW scene for people to think that earlier is better, and owners never seem to be content: if you own a late model Bug, then a pre-'68 one seems a more attractive proposition; owners of Bay Window Buses covet Split-Screens; and Split Screen owners want an earlier model still – perhaps a pre-'55 Barndoor.

Some people go even further: they flip a car (from the USA to Europe for instance), and get a taste for it, realising they can fund their hobby this way, or set-up a successful business doing what they love. I know lots of guys, including myself, who have quit their (boring)

Rising prices and rarity of good cars hitting the market now forces people to take on bigger projects; after skilful repair and paint blending, you'd never know Jeff Laughlin's car once looked like the top picture. (Courtesy Jeff Laughlin)

Late model cars were once largely ignored and dubbed as 'Fat chicks' in the USA; Austin Working's factory black '68 with hardcore Patina proves they can look awesome with the correct treatment. (Courtesy Derek 'Boxrod' Campbell)

Johnny Montana's '61 was a Swedish Barn Find, and the subject of a year-long preservation project; many wouldn't realise a car like this hasn't been restored. (Author's collection)

service items or restoration parts. Supplies of good original parts or New Old Stock (NOS), that have lived on the shelves of dealers or collectors for decades, are either drying up or being hoarded by some collectors, either in the hope of naming their price in the future, or just because they love Volkswagens and anything associated with them.

Some collectors are lucky to have one of everything, but nothing is for sale, and they often face criticism for this. Yes, most of their cars and parts may spend the rest of their lives in a dusty collection, away from prying eyes, never to see the light of day again, but I believe that the people who condemn these so-called hoarders are missing the point. If you have the money to fill your life with classic memorabilia, then that is entirely your prerogative; anyone getting annoyed about this is usually envious.

Then there are the serial car builders, those who buy vehicles that others pass up, and bring them back to life. This is very time-consuming work but many of these guys seemingly build car after car without any gaps. They build cars in their free time, so, disregarding the number of man hours they spend on a car, it's possible to sell them for a profit; when done, they move straight on to the next one. With this approach, the serial car builder can move up the ranks pretty fast, going on to own progressively rarer and higher value vehicles. More than just a hobby, this is a lifestyle.

While some serial car builders build cars just for the thrill of it – profit is often a handy bi-product – there

jobs to make money out of old Volkswagens, whether it's dealing in cars or parts, offering a service, or turning them into trendy coffee or food trucks.

There are many in the scene who would rather that these cars were still less popular, and therefore more affordable, but the problem with this is that no one would then be willing to reproduce body panels, are also some serious VW businesses that have always championed Patina cars and understand what it takes to build a cool looking car, without giving it a repaint. Some of these pro builders are restoration shops, who have the skills to build 100-point restored show cars, but they favour Patina cars when it comes to their own drive, or at least have an interest in Patina cars, so are happy to build them for their customers.

Of course, with many guys dabbling in both collecting and dealing, the distinction between the roles people play can get a little blurred; with all of this in mind, let's take a look inside the garages, workshops and collections of some of the faces behind some of the world's best VW Patina cars.

The Collectors
Gibbs Connors
Gibbs' love of Volkswagens started at a very young age with a yellow Tonka Bug toy car. When the time came to get a real car, there was only one choice, and he ended up with a hand-me-down yellow '72 Bug from his sister. This was back in 1979 when used Bugs would still show up on the Volkswagen dealer's used car lot, which was where Gibbs' second Bug, also yellow, was purchased.

For hardcore Volkswagen guys, collecting is not just about the cars; Gibbs Connors has built up an impressive collection of toys, parts, and memorabilia, including several cool old signs.
(Courtesy Shin Watanabe)

Gibbs Connors got into Volkswagens by way of a yellow Bug Tonka toy. (Courtesy Shin Watanabe)

Gibbs Connors' 'Jurassic Barndoor' has amazing original Patina all over the surface of the bodywork; he added to the look by lowering it with a narrowed front beam and Randar wheels. (Courtesy Shin Watanabe)

The 'King Panel' was discovered local to Gibbs' Philadelphia home; it had been sold new at a dealership a few blocks away and the phone number is still in use by the original owner's sister. (Courtesy Shin Watanabe)

Gibbs had a thing for original Hurst bumpers for a long time and amassed quite a collection; they were originally manufactured locally to where he lives. (Courtesy Gibbs Connors)

Originally a Swedish car, Gibbs' Split Beetle is one of the nicest original Survivor Split Bugs on the planet. The suspension modifications are fully reversible. (Courtesy Shin Watanabe)

Fast forward to 1993, and Gibbs bought his first Bus, a '63 Single Cab Truck, from an advert at the back of *Hot VWs* magazine; the truck was in Oklahoma, and it took a year and a half (pre-internet days) to get it shipped to his home in Pennsylvania. From that first Split Truck, a passion developed and, as for many guys, earlier, rarer, or more historically significant vehicles would trump what he owned at the time, tempting him to buy and sell a lot of cars until he was happy with his collection.

Gibbs has traded up over the years, owning everything from late Split Buses to early pressed Bumper Buses, a Binz Double Cab, and a few Barndoor Buses too. As well as collecting Buses, he has amassed an impressive collection of good original and NOS parts too. He developed a penchant for original Bus middle seats and Hurst bumpers for a while; usually removed from Buses and disposed of over the years, these are now rare and hard to find in good original condition. Everyone who is into Patina cars seems to have a different approach to what drives them, but when it comes to Gibbs, it has to be original, above all else: "The Patina thing, it's original paint to me; the originality and preservation is all that matters."

Bob Van Heyst – BBT

Bob founded BBT, with partner Arlette, in Belgium in 1986, with a 20m² workshop and three pallet loads of parts sourced from the USA. When his first customers turned up from different countries, Bob knew that he was onto something. As parts began to overflow from the workshop and his parent's attic, he moved to a new space, double the size. Four years later, he moved again to a purpose-built industrial unit.

For many years, BBT worked out of the same industrial unit in Sint Job In't Goor, near Antwerp, Belgium; as the business, and Bob's collection of air-cooled VWs, expanded, so did the unit, with an extension added in 2003. In 2011, Bob and Arlette moved BBT around the corner, on the same industrial park, to a 4200m² state of the art unit, part of which now houses Bob's own private collection of cars and his 'Virgin Outlaws.'

Bob stands proudly with some of his favourite cars in front of his VW parts shop in Belgium, including a very rare Double Door Walkthru 23-window Deluxe Microbus. (Courtesy Bob Van Heyst)

Bob Van Heyst has amassed one of the most interesting private VW collections anywhere. Bob showcases his own cars alongside his 'Virgin Outlaw' cars which are for sale. (Courtesy Bob Van Heyst)

Bob, who has always had a thing for 'first paint' cars, coined the phrase: "You can paint a lot of fun out of a car." (Courtesy Bob Van Heyst)

An original paint Sealing Wax Red Split Bus for sale by Bob some years ago at Le Bug Show in Spa, Belgium. (Author's collection)

Bob specialises in sourcing original 'first paint' cars from around the world; these sit inside the same facility as his own private cars and are for sale. If you're looking for an original paint Volkswagen, then a trip to BBT will definitely be worthwhile. What's more, you'll be able to view Bob's private collection at the same time as looking for a car of your own. Bob is a very friendly and hospitable guy, even opening the doors to his shop and museum, laying on food and camping, for visitors attending Bad Camberg and Hessisch Oldendorf vintage shows.

From rare cars to dealer signs and original Volkswagen cutaway display cars, Bob's collection has it all. (Author's collection)

Today, Bob is as enthusiastic about Volkswagens as he has ever been. As well as collecting rare cars, he's the proud owner of an eccentric collection of Spilt Beetle radios: Telefunken, Blaupunkt, and Becker amongst others. Bob also has a collection of rare steering wheels, enamel signs, old dealer signs, and cool accessories from the '50s and '60s. These days, when Bob isn't working or playing with his toys, he'll more than likely be reading his huge collection of Volkswagen literature, parts books, and workshop manuals.

Bob's private car collection includes: a '43 Schwimmwagen; a '44 Kübelwagen; a '56 Denzel; two Split Window Bugs from '49 and '50; a '56 Porsche Speedster; a '52 and a '54 Porsche 356 Convertible; a '49 Hebmuller (no. 56); a '52 Karmann Convertible; a '52 Rometsch four-door Taxi; a '53 Zwitter Ragtop; a '51 and '54 Barndoor Bus; a '58 original paint Double Door Walkthru 23-window Samba; a '58, '59 and '63 Westfalia; a '57 Karmann Ghia lowlight Coupé with 356 mechanicals; a '58 and '59 Karmann Ghia Lowlight Convertible; a '62 Type 34; a '64 Type 3 Notchback; a '65 Double Cab Pickup; and a '65 Ladder Truck. There's also a couple of

Johnny Montana in awe of Bob Van Heyst's collection on a trip to Belgium with the author in 2012. (Author's collection)

cool motorcycles, a few vintage bikes, and, of course, a lot of toys.

Being involved almost his whole life with Volkswagens, day in, day out, Bob loves Patina and originality the most; he's not a fan of made up Patina or Fauxtina, but all-original Patina created by time and Mother Nature. "Pure cars," he calls them. His search for perfect Patina cars and parts takes him all over the globe, always hunting down cool cars; very few are still found in barns and fields, others are picked up from collectors.

"Old cars should look old," is Bob's reply when people ask him why he likes Patina. The main reason he likes them so much is that "when they're nicely sorted out they're so much fun to drive." Bob used to own several, top quality, restored cars but he says they're harder to drive, worrying about ruining them the more you use them.

One of my favourite ever quotes about Patina, from Bob, is: "You can paint a lot of fun out of a car."

Lin Ottinger

Lin's collection came about as a result of his business: Lin Ottinger's Rock Shop. The shop has been a feature of downtown Moab, Utah since 1960, and soon after it opened he began giving guided tours of, what is now, Canyonlands National Park. His vehicle of choice for the tours? A VW 23-window Deluxe Microbus. Ottinger would buy the Buses in used condition and carry out some subtle modifications: rear bumpers were removed and rear corners radiused, then the air intake would be ducted up through the back of the roof. These modifications made it possible to go off the beaten track, and further into the parks. As his tours became more popular, with locals and tourists alike, his fleet of Buses expanded.

The Deluxe Buses were perfect for Ottinger's tours. Passengers could stand up in the back with the sunroof wide open – Ottinger fitted original Bus grab handles just in front of the Sunroof so they could hang on. With his fleet of seven deluxe 21 and 23-window

Lin Ottinger bought all his Buses as cheap used cars to run tours of the Utah National Parks. The Buses received modifications for extra ground clearance and a roof mounted air intake. (Courtesy Ottinger Family)

Each Bus was used extensively for 20 years in the parks, before being stored first in an open compound, and later in the warehouse. (Courtesy Ottinger Family)

All six Buses on the mezzanine are in the same condition as when they were parked, except they have more Patina from years stored in the searing Moab heat. (Courtesy Joanna Cooke/Departure PR)

Top: Lin and Sonny Ottinger's car collection is eclectic, to say the least, but it's the Buses that hold pride of place; they signify an exciting time in the Ottinger family history. Bottom, left to right: the author, John Jones, Rusty Willey, and Lin Ottinger. (Both courtesy Joanna Cooke/Departure PR)

Buses, he continued hosting tours until the 1980s, before parking them in the compound of his shop at 600 N Main Street.

"People would jump the fence and steal parts off them, so we moved them out of town into a warehouse; now they're locked away from prying eyes," said Lin.

They remained stowed away until John Jones of KCW made Lin an offer he couldn't refuse. John had bought Lin's crashed 23-window Barndoor Bus from a local junkyard owner a few years before (his daughter accidentally drove the Bus off a cliff in 1967, sustaining bad roof damage). Although the Bus was bought by John from the junkyard, for a large sum of money, as far as Lin was concerned, he was still the rightful owner. To try and make amends, John offered to trailer one of Lin's buses, from his tour fleet, to his KCW shop in Grand Junction and carry out a full mechanical restoration at his own cost.

The completed Bus was delivered back to Lin in time for the Moab car show of 2016; to give thanks to John, Lin and his son, Sonny Ottinger, invited John and friends to camp at the warehouse. This was the first time anyone had been allowed inside the warehouse to see Lin's historic fleet of Buses since they were stored away. I had a chance to meet Lin in early 2018, and being able to climb up onto the mezzanine floor and look around seven original paint, logoed Deluxe Buses was an honour and a dream come true.

While many are quick to accuse Lin of 'hoarding' (the Buses aren't for sale, at any price) Lin and Sonny value the Buses as part of their family history – the golden years of their business – and rightly want to hang on to them. Lin is now in his 90s but still works in The Rock Shop every day. Sonny plans to get each and every Bus in the warehouse back into roadworthy condition, and back on display to the public one day.

Jason Smurthwaite of Utah-based Westy Restorations recommissioned one of Lin's original Buses a couple of years ago, to join the one that John Jones of KCW got back on the road a few years prior. Note the exhaust stack exiting the rear of the roof, and no rear bumper for better ground clearance. (Courtesy Westy Restorations)

Cody not only has a thing for original paint cars, but also collects original paint wheels from the era before wheel colours were standardised; thanks to an accommodating better half, these are kept on display in his home. (Courtesy Cody Goss)

Small details like this original VW dealer service reminder, as shown on Cody Goss' '61 'Mabel,' are just one of the things you won't see on a freshly restored car, as all traces of usage are wiped out forever. (Courtesy Cody Goss)

Far from locking his cars away dry and safe from winter weather, Cody Goss uses his '61 year-round, taking many extended trips during the harsh Idaho winters. (Courtesy Cody Goss)

Cody Goss

Cody started out slamming every VW he owned; his 1958 Bug was driven at stock height for a while before being super-slammed with a transmission raise, flat floorpans, and air ride. As Cody put it: "I saw the error of my ways," and he began returning the car to stock, including restoring the hacked out rear package tray. The car has also been stripped back to the original L245 Light Bronze paint.

Cody also now owns an amazing original paint L456 Ruby Red Bug which he drives year-round in all weathers. For the last five years, Cody has also been collecting pre-1966 original paint wheels; before '66, Volkswagen would match wheel colours to the body colour, with a contrasting colour added to the rim or wheel centre, depending on the year of manufacture. Cody has quite an impressive collection of wheels, including a full set of original paint wheels for both his cars.

Chadd Magee

Chadd lives in Georgia, USA, and what hasn't passed through his hands, in terms of both cars and parts over the years, probably isn't worth owning. Together with his partner, Kat, Chadd is a collector, dealer, and serial builder of cool Volkswagens, and has an enviable collection of cars in his current stable. He sources and sells cars and rare parts worldwide and always has a project or three on the go. Chadd famously built the hardcore clearcoated green Patina car for actor Ewan McGregor.

Lots of people in the Patina VW scene love original aftermarket parts from the '50s and '60s, and Chadd is no exception; over the past 20 years, he has built up possibly the largest collection of original VW

Just a small selection of the rare VW aftermarket wheels which Chadd Magee owns, as displayed at the 2010 Florida Winterjam. (Courtesy Chadd Magee)

A RHD car which Chadd imported from the UK some time ago, the '64 Type 34 Karmann Ghia is super slammed on Fuchs wheels, and now resides with Chadd in Atlanta, Georgia. (Courtesy Alexis Peraza)

'Pedro the Bay' was built by Chadd and Kat in late 2017. A Brilliant Blue 1970 Deluxe, Pedro has a great look, especially with the fairly uncommon, polished Speedmaster wheels. (Courtesy Chadd Magee)

'Terry the Turk' is an L380 Turkis '63 Ragtop that Chadd and partner Kat built. Finished in 2018, Kat decided to do something a little different with the interior on this car. (Courtesy Chadd Magee)

aftermarket wheels in the world, some of which are for sale. He is also well known for restoring vintage wheels too.

Chadd Magee began collecting and selling VW parts many years ago and has built up quite a collection of cars and parts from the '60s and '70s. He got the chance to display a large amount of rare aftermarket wheels and parts at the 2010 Florida Winterjam, such as these rare gear shifters. (Courtesy Chadd Magee)

Chadd favours clearcoating on his hardcore Patina cars; he built this 1960 Ceramic Green Ragtop some time ago and sold it to actor Ewan McGregor. (Courtesy Chadd Magee)

The Prolific Patina Car Builders
Craig Yelley

Craig got into VWs with his first car, a '61 Bug that he push-started every day for a year until he figured out how to fix it. In 1995, after a car accident, he needed to find something to fill his recovery time. He paid $120 for ten cars, in pieces, out of someone's yard, and built one good car out of them. Having put every cent he had into finishing that car so he could sell it, Craig turned a good profit and his shop – Vintage VW in Spokane, Washington was born.

This original paint Mango Green/Seagull Grey Bus was repainted white when Craig got hold of it; he painstakingly stripped it back to original. As there is now a fair bit of surface rust, Craig clearcoated the Bus. (Courtesy Craig Yelley)

Craig Yelley has been prolifically building Buses for over 25 years, and usually favours the polished Patina look. This Palm Green/Sand Green Microbus dictated its own look, though, and was slammed on BTR Racing wheels, which take a lot of work to tuck inside the original bodywork. (Courtesy Craig Yelley)

More recently, Craig has built a few more stock height Bay Window Buses; his formula includes rust repair, paint blending, and buffing the original paint to a mirror-like shine. (Courtesy Craig Yelley)

Craig has prolifically built cool Buses over the last 20 plus years; in the '90s everything he built would be immediately snapped up by Japanese buyers, but nowadays his Buses go all over the world. The thing that sets Craig's builds apart from other builders, is that he specialises in sympathetically restoring Patina Buses, and will quite often carry out a lot of metal repair, but then carefully blend in the paint to look

original. In recent years, due to the rarity of good Split project Buses, Craig has built a lot of Bay Window Buses, too.

Jason Reich
Well known within the Southern California VW scene, Jason is another prolific builder of cool Patina VWs. He has the flair to give each car the right look; every

I first heard about Jason Reich when Kustom Coach Werks lowered his original paint Barndoor Standard Microbus on Fuchs wheels many years ago. (Courtesy Jason Reich/Aircooled Vintage Works)

car he builds sits just right, with the right amount of Patina and the coolest wheels and accessories. From '60s Bugs to Patina Barndoor Buses, Jason has built, bought, and sold them all. He got into VWs in 1996 with a 'Horrible' '65 Bug that had all the fenders bondoed onto the body; he soon gave this away, before buying a 1956 Bug, then a '55 Ragtop Bug.

After fully restoring a 1950 Split Beetle, Jason began to see the attraction of original paint cars: "The restored '50 made me focus on imperfections. I realised it could never be perfect and I was also scared to use it; it drove me crazy." There then began a period of buying and building original paint cars, culminating in his current collection: a 1957 Kombi with original faded logos; a '51 Porsche 356; and a Patina Chevy Truck.

Jason's original paint '58 Euro Ragtop Beetle ran original EMPI Sprint Star Wheels and was featured in *VolksWorld* magazine. (Courtesy Jason Reich/Aircooled Vintage Works)

Jason's '63 Bug was given a full restoration inside and underneath. The original Ruby Red paint was polished, but Jason was still too precious about driving what was now a show car. (Courtesy Jason Reich/Aircooled Vintage Works)

The 'Model Laundry' Kombi is Jason's newest project; he plans to make it into a nice original paint driver. (Courtesy Jason Reich/Aircooled Vintage Works)

Jason ran this slammed Barndoor Pickup on original Superior wheels as a daily driver for over a year. (Courtesy Jason Reich/Aircooled Vintage Works)

The 'Finks Laundry' Barndoor Standard was just another cool logo Bus built by Andre Burchard, who has now learned to sympathetically re-touch logos himself. (Courtesy Andre Burchard)

Unlike some, who seem to build cars and keep them forever, Jason seems to excel in building cars and selling them to build another. His most recent project was a very nice original paint L456 Ruby Red 1963 Bug; it was in amazing original condition, with a mild lowering job when Jason bought it, but was soon in a million pieces as he restored every last nut and bolt of the car to show condition underneath, whilst just polishing the original paint on the top side of the body to a mirror finish. The car was sold soon after completion. Why? "It was too perfect to use."

Andre Burchard

I first learned of Andre when he bought the 'Bob Hammond' Barndoor Panel from a fellow forum user on thesamba.com. This incredibly rare Barndoor Walkthru Panel had been discovered on a property in the USA and repainted in black. Andre stepped in and what happened next was a Bus preservation-type restoration of the highest order; he carried out some major metal repairs underneath and successfully stripped off the black repaint to expose nice original paint and faded logos.

To do the restoration of the Bus justice, he enlisted the help of Dennis, a local traditional sign painter, to sympathetically re-touch the logos. Andre decided long ago that lowering wasn't for him, so the Bus was mechanically restored to stock condition. The 'Bob Hammond' Bus was a landmark build for him. Building Buses was nothing new – he owned his first Patina Bus in 2003 after being inspired by Brendan

Andre has built a fair few original logo Buses; his most recent is the 'Barrett Bros Music Box' Bus. (Courtesy Andre Burchard)

The 'Bob Hammond' Panel was painted black over the original paint when it was discovered and was one of only two known Barndoor Walkthru Buses known at the time. Andre Burchard carefully stripped it back to original paint and had a local sign painter re-touch the logos. (Courtesy Mike Johnson)

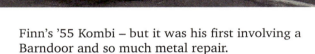

Finn's '55 Kombi – but it was his first involving a Barndoor and so much metal repair.

Once the Hammond Bus was done, however, Andre soon found the lure of another project too good to pass up; he's since prolifically bought, built, and sold many more Buses, Bugs, and Karmann Ghias, and, despite being happy with his current collection of cars, he's still always working on another project, with others waiting in the wings.

Ben Laughton
I first heard of Ben when I'd bought the remains of a '51 Barndoor Bus in 2011. I'd seen the Bus on a trip out to Sundsvall, Sweden, where I'd gone to collect a '69 Bay Window Bus I'd bought on the internet. When I arrived, the vendor collected me from the airport in an all-original

No stranger to Swedish forest find Buses, Ben Laughton takes on projects that many think are beyond restoration. (Courtesy Ben Laughton)

Ben Laughton loves huge project Buses and specialises in Barndoor builds. The 'Quality Sound' Barndoor Deluxe was cut up with a gas torch in the 1980s after a minor rear end shunt. (Courtesy Ben Laughton)

The 'Quality Sound' Bus was pieced back together, using as much original metal as possible; it was sympathetically paint blended and it's hard to tell now that it was once in pieces. (Courtesy Ben Laughton)

'51 Karmann Cabriolet and took me back to his home, where he had VW treasures galore. The remains of the '51 Barndoor had been dragged out of Swedish woodland, having already had a lot of parts – such as the front of the roof – cut off. The Bus still had all its numbers and Swedish paperwork, so I agreed to buy it for 5000 SEK (around £500 or $300 at the time). When I arrived home and put a couple of pictures on thesamba.com forums, I received a call from Ben during which he offered me a decent sum of money to deliver the Bus to him.

Ben put that '51 back on the road and it eventually made its way back to Sweden, but for Ben it was just the latest in a long line of mega saves, featuring Buses that many people thought were beyond help. Quite how Ben has the enthusiasm and foresight to resurrect many of these Buses, I have no idea, but at any one time, he usually has at least a couple of major projects on the go. Hats off to you Ben, for all the rare Buses you've helped to save.

The Commission Dealers
Brendan Finn
Although many gained their love of old VWs from growing up around them, Brendan Finn can go one better; his mother swears he was conceived in the back of the family's Anthracite Grey 1962 Beetle. After this early start, and growing up around air-cooled VWs, he turned to Split Windscreen Buses when the time came to get his own wheels: "It was the mid-'80s and I was looking for my first car; I used to surf and skate a lot, and back then an old Split Windshield Bus was

the coolest car you could get for the money. They were perfect for storing boards in the back too."

From these early beginnings, Brendan majored in English at San Diego State; it taught him how to communicate well and harness the power of the written word. It was his flair for writing that led his friends to ask him to sell their Buses for them; he knew a lot about VWs, the people and the market, having been involved in the scene for years. Word spread, and before long selling buses for others had become a good side earner, until it really took off and began to be a hindrance to his day job.

Today, Brendan sells high-value Classic VWs full-time, but always maintains a huge degree of integrity; he won't take on just any car to sell, it has to be of some historical significance and he prides himself on full disclosure of a vehicle's faults, as well as knowing all the year-correct details. Over the last ten years, while selling other people's Buses, there hasn't

What Brendan Finn doesn't know about specific model year changes, especially on Barndoor Buses, probably isn't worth knowing. Brendan has owned this Survivor Barndoor Panel for many years. (Courtesy Brendan Finn)

Brendan's old 1955 Kombi inspired the author, and many others, back in 2003, to build slammed original paint buses: it's now owned by Steve Op De Beeck in Belgium but retains the exact same look. (Courtesy Steve Op De Beeck)

been much change in his own collection; he did what many have done, buying and selling several 'stepping stone' cars before settling on his current crop of favourites.

Perhaps surprisingly, especially when you consider he owns a 1953 Barndoor logo panel Bus and a 'Time Capsule' original paint Barndoor Standard Bus, the one he'd never, ever part with is his all-original, 34,000-mile 1960 L345 Light Grey Kombi. Brendan recalls first seeing this Bus sitting on jack stands a few houses down from the house he moved into at age five, in 1977. It took him 11 years of pursuing before he finally became its second owner: he eventually bought it from the estate sale.

The final jewel in Brendan's personal collection is an original paint 1959 seamed gate Double Cab

Brendan first saw this all-original 1960 L345 Light Grey Kombi up on jack stands when he moved to the neighbourhood at age five. He actively pursued this 34,000-mile Survivor for 11 years. (Courtesy Brendan Finn)

Brendan's latest find is this all-original 1959 seamed gate Double Cab. It sat in Butte, Montana for many years, and was sold new at Evel Knievel's grandfather's VW dealership in Butte. (Courtesy Brendan Finn)

Pickup, which sat in Butte, Montana since the 1970s; the truck has a load of one-year-only features, as well as a few oddities which confounded all but long-time Bus collector Charlie Hamill. One of the things that makes the truck extra special is the fact that it was sold new at Evel Knievel's grandfather's Volkswagen dealership in Butte, Montana. For a kid growing up in the '70s, with Evel Knievel toys, this fact adds a very cool story to this amazing vehicle.

Randy Carlson
A famous face in the California VW scene, Randy has been running oldbug.com for many years. Through Oldbug, Randy offers commission selling for high-quality classic Volkswagens; his aim is to only sell cars that he would want to buy himself, and is always transparent with details of the car, warts and all, so customers can buy through his website with complete confidence. "My father once told me, 'never buy a car that you wouldn't want to keep forever,' so when folks bring us cars to advertise, I keep that in mind – if a car has major flaws, then I tend to steer clear of it."

Randy's reputation, and popularity, when it comes to cars, VWs in particular, has led to several TV opportunities over the years; he's appeared on shows such as *Monster Garage*, *Lords of the Car Hoards*, *Jay Leno's Garage*, and, more recently, as the appraiser on Discovery Channel's *Sticker Shock*, where the team investigate the history and condition of a wide range of vehicles to help determine their true value. Randy lives in Southern California and has quite a collection of cars, many of them being quirky or eclectic; he is also the founder of Carchaeology, a vintage vehicle rescue and preservation group.

Randy Carlson was lucky enough to become the new owner of 'Randy's VW'; the original owner, Randy Pollack, operated a VW wrecking yard in Central California and would drive his 'Show Car' to VW events all across the state. The car famously featured in an episode of *American Pickers*, when Mike Wolfe and Frank Fritz visited Randy. (Courtesy Randy Carlson)

Randy Carlson on 'Randy's VW': "The car and Randy were together … the car being the mechanical version of Randy and Randy being the human form of the car – reliable, entertaining, and a little rough around the edges." (Courtesy Randy Carlson)

John Jones' 23-window Barndoor after being massaged back into shape; there are only a handful of people in the VW scene who could have repaired this Bus without compromising the Patina. (Courtesy Derek 'Boxrod' Campbell)

The Pro Builder
John Jones

John runs Kustom Coach Werks (KCW) in Grand Junction, Colorado. He founded the company in 2001, and is one of the most prolific VW restorers of all time. I first heard about KCW through thesamba.com back in 2003. John was doing a full body-off restoration on a Bug and, to promote his company, he ran the project on the forum of his own website – www.kustomcoachwerks.com – calling it 'The 45-Day Wonder.' Considering every part of this car was dismantled, restored, painted, and detailed, it was a surprise when John finished the build in just 26 days.

Bearing in mind that most VW restoration shops, the world over, will often take years to complete a full restoration (many others take longer), this made John's feat even more impressive. If this was just one car build, a publicity stunt to win more business, then perhaps working day and night to complete it could be understood, but this is actually just how John works.

Over the last 17 years, the KCW team have prolifically turned out more show quality restorations than any other company in the world. What's more,

John Jones' much fabled Barndoor Deluxe as purchased, having fallen off a cliff in 1967 while being used on a Canyonlands tour by Lin Ottinger's daughter. (Courtesy John Jones/Kustom Coach Werks)

every part of the restoration of these cars is shown, with full transparency, on the KCW website and forum.

While fully restored cars were John's bread and butter in the early days, and in some respects, even now, he was also a key player in Patina cars being popularised and was instrumental – by employing Derrick Pacheco for a while – in the beginnings of the Hoodride movement.

John Jones (on the left) with 'Big Dizzle' in the 'Dumped Pumpkin'; one of the first KCW/Hoodride builds back in 2004. (Courtesy John Jones/ Kustom Coach Werks)

Kustom Coach Werks has everything they need in-house to carry out full restorations and Patina builds; it is, without a doubt, the most prolific VW restoration shop in the world. (Author's collection)

More recently, John and the KCW crew have built themselves stock height or raised Buses; John's '55 'Pamper' is a solid road-tripper, having been driven as far as Colorado to Mexico, and back. (Author's collection)

Indeed, since around 2004, John has built just as many Patina cars as shiny show cars for both customers and his own collection. KCW was founded on a 'sweat of my brow' work ethic, and John continues to personify his company mantra: 'Effort and sacrifice, passion and drive.' This has led to him building a house in the grounds of his workshop, working up to 20 hours a day to get cars finished. When he's not cranking on customers' cars he's often found building several personal projects each year.

Through his amazing work, John has won a lot of repeat business and can proudly call many of his loyal customers his personal friends. Whilst researching for this book, I was generously offered an all-expenses-paid trip to visit KCW and meet John; a dream come true after following his work for 15 years. After visiting, and seeing the setup, I now understand how KCW manage to build so many great cars; it is a very well-oiled machine. More than this though, John, his wife, Gretchen, and the KCW team's character and spirit endear them to everyone they meet. I really like that they allow customers to get involved, truly making dreams a reality – 'Building Dreams Daily.'

When it comes to personal car builds, John has owned more than a few Patina Buses and trucks; he currently owns a 1955 Panel Bus that was stripped back to original paint, rust repaired, and left to season in the dry Grand Junction climate.

Where once all KCW built cars were slammed

Having built a few body dropped Buses already over the years, the 'Abbott Cleaners' Bus was a more recent T2D Patina build.
(Courtesy Type 2 Detectives)

T2D don't just build cool Buses, as this slammed Patina Lowlight Karmann Ghia on 17in Fuchs shows.
(Courtesy Type 2 Detectives)

suspension – either static or air ride – cars are being built to be used on all terrains; stock height Buses and Baja Bugs are the norm at John's shop these days. John and the crew live and breathe VWs, seven days a week. It's work *and* play, and they think nothing of road-tripping cross-country to VW shows and campouts to catch up with friends.

Type 2 Detectives

Paul Medhurst began Type 3 Detectives (T3D) in the 1990s, after a stint working for Ritchie King at Karmann Konnection. Specialising for many years in sourcing, restoring, and finding parts for the Type 3 range, he had a number of magazine-featured cars and became well known in the UK VW scene. As Buses gained popularity, Paul later formed Type 2 Detectives (T2D), which he ran alongside T3D for a few years, before deciding to go it alone with T2D, and bring a business partner, Mark Fulton, on board.

Continuing in the early vane of T3D, T2D has built a lot of magazine-featured cars and Buses, with many of them being of the Patina variety; T2D became famous for radical suspension modifications, pushing the boundaries when it came to slamming VWs. They're also well known for body dropping Buses – channelling the body over the chassis to make them sit virtually on the floor. Recently, Paul and his team have worked with TV production companies, have moved to larger premises, with a huge car showroom, and have moved away from suspension modifications to provide 'bootcamp' workshops for car owners wanting to get more involved in maintenance and repair.

Evil Ben's

Ben Lewis first became famous in the UK VW scene for building a couple of magazine featured cars; notably 'Fendered 57,' an Oval Window Bug painted in VW Mango Green with rare Foxcraft rear fender skirts fitted. Fendered 57 was insanely detailed, and went on to win at numerous shows. Many years ago, Ben decided to relocate to Cornwall, UK, where he worked for another VW garage for a while, before leaving to start-up Evil Ben's in early 2009.

With a reputation for high-quality metal repair and detailed work, Evil Ben's is behind many magazine-quality cars, and is a member of the UK German Folks Klub (GFK). Notable amongst Ben's car builds are Mike Attewell's RHD oval dash Karmann Cabriolet, which took

Ben Lewis always likes to push the boundaries with his personal builds; his super-slammed VW Australia Country Buggy blew everyone away at *VolksWorld* show a few years ago and was featured in *Ultra VW* magazine. (Courtesy Keith Seume)

Ben Lewis' '71 Bay Window Bus is a regular at UK VW shows and rides low courtesy of air ride suspension. The author wrote a feature about this Bus for *VolksWorld* magazine in 2014. (Courtesy Joss Ashley)

Mike Attewell's original oval dash Karmann Cabriolet was built at Evil Ben's and featured on the cover of *VolksWorld* magazine; it featured a six-inch narrowed beam and air ride. The car subsequently got restored. (Courtesy *VolksWorld*)

Chase Hill has several high-quality car builds under his belt and now manufactures his own range of suspension products, from extended trailing arms to Bus wheel tubs. (Courtesy Shin Watanabe)

the world by storm a few years ago, as well as his own super-slammed Australian VW Country Buggy. While many of Evil Ben's builds are full show-quality restorations, these days Ben can be seen driving Patina cars; his super-slammed Bay Window Westfalia Camper was featured in *VolksWorld* a few years ago and is well known on the VW scene.

Chase Hill – Cage 66

I first learned about Chase through various internet forums back in the Hoodride days. Chase had an early Mango Green project Bus and was determined to build it without buying any off-the-shelf suspension products; he made his own drop spindles, narrowed beam, and adjustable rear spring plates amongst other things. As time went on, Chase continued to build his own project cars, while developing a line of unique products for really low Volkswagens; he manufactures his own raised front wheel tubs for Buses, and makes extended front trailing arms to help centre the front wheels in the wheelarches on lowered Bugs.

The Website Guru
Everett Barnes – www.thesamba.com

Thesamba.com (TS), founded in 1997 by Everett Barnes, has grown into the largest and most dynamic air-cooled Volkswagen community online today. In the early days of the Internet, Everett just wanted a

Founded in 1997 by Everett Barnes, thesamba.com is the biggest air-cooled VW website in the world, featuring everything from free classified adverts to a gallery, forums, and archive material. (Courtesy Everett Barnes)

place to post his growing collection of VW photos and literature online. Now, with more than 1.6 million gallery photos, more than 100,000 free classified ads, and over seven million forum posts, TS has gained a global audience of Volkswagen enthusiasts, with over 50,000 unique daily visitors. In addition, the site currently includes an extensive archive of Volkswagen literature and manuals, a huge technical reference section, and worldwide listings for VW-related events, clubs, links, and businesses.

Basically, if you're into vintage Volkswagens, you need to be part of TS.

Everett has owned a lot of VWs over the last 20 years; his current collection includes an all original factory black '63 Squareback, and an incredible Sealing Wax Red Patina '61 Double Cab Pickup.

Like many people, Everett has traded up his cars over the years, to the point where he is happy with his collection; Everett's '61 L53 Sealing Wax Red Double Cab has amazing original Patina. (Courtesy Everett Barnes)

The Magazine Guys
Niels 'Airmighty' Timmerman

Niels is based in The Netherlands, and set up his Airmighty website many years ago; it was one of the best places to go if you wanted great pictures from practically every Volkswagen show in Europe and the USA. As the website became more and more popular, and took up more of Niels' time, he decided to launch *Airmighty Megascene* magazine in January 2010, together with fellow VW guy Kobus Cantraine.

An exclusive, high-end quarterly publication, *Airmighty Megascene* is printed in English as the lead language but is also translated into German and French. If you're looking for high-quality photos covering the best VWs and VW events

Like holding a book in your hands: *Airmighty* is a high quality publication, packed with outstanding air-cooled VW features. (Author's collection)

globally, this magazine won't disappoint. What's more, the quality of the paper and glossy printing makes these 'magazines' seem more like a book, and are definitely worth collecting.

Paul Knight's old Type 181 Trekker had great patina; it was slammed on JGE Rader wheels. The photo is taken on the Essex Riviera – Southend on Sea. (Courtesy Paul Knight)

Volksworld was putting patina cars on the front cover way before it was fashionable to do so; it helped that editors James Peene and Paul Knight both love patina cars. (Author's collection)

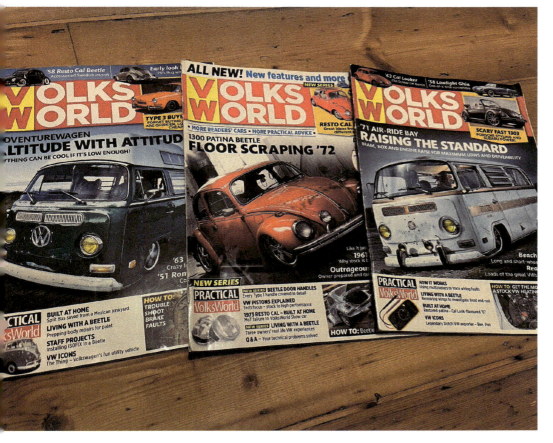

VolksWorld Magazine

The longest-running magazine in the UK, *VolksWorld* was first published in 1987, with Keith Seume as founding editor. Over the years, the magazine has championed patina cars, beginning with putting the Linde Bus on the cover in the mid-'90s when most people didn't get what patina was all about.

Current editor Paul Knight was one of the main people banging the patina drum in the early days; he left to edit *Ultra VW* magazine for many years, but when *Ultra* was eventually sold to the current owner of *VolksWorld*, Paul ended up in the *VolksWorld* editor's chair.

The Young Gun
Jake Hilling/HR Autoworks

Just as some are getting worried that everyone in the VW scene is getting older and there isn't enough fresh blood on the scene, along come guys like Jake Hilling and his company HR Autoworks. At the tender age of 24, Jake has built a successful business off the back of serious blood, sweat and tears. He restored his first Beetle with his dad Gary at the tender age of 14, then the pair discovered a patina Oval Beetle on a trip to Florida, and the HR formula for patina restorations began.

Jake started HR in 2016 with a unit in Hampshire, but then relocated to workshops at the bottom of his parent's garden when the first unit was lost. He now has a team of guys and they prolifically build cars; every single one is built from the ground up – in many ways over-restored underneath, but always with a patina look unique to the base vehicle on the outside. This means that all HR cars are built to last, with a full running gear refresh and painted undersides to look factory fresh.

Jake and his team seem to build Beetles prolifically; this Pastel Green Split Beetle proudly still wears a lot of surface rust, despite being like a new car underneath. (Courtesy Jake Hilling/HR Autoworks)

This Ragtop Beetle is typical of the style of build that HR turn out; every car is built from the ground up and features seriously low (usually static) suspension. (Courtesy Jake Hilling/HR Autoworks)

A more recent build of Jake's, this L31 Dove Blue Single Cab really has the look. It's slammed over Cosmic wheels with clearcoated paintwork. (Courtesy Martin 'Chuff' Wall)

Jake has family connections in Portugal, and that's where a lot of his project vehicles come from, such as this L380 Turkis Beetle, which looks a world away from how it did when Jake first imported it. (Courtesy Jake Hilling/HR Autoworks)

With links to Portugal and the USA, Jake finds plenty of hardcore patina cars each year, some of which he advertises as project cars, but he's beginning to find that most people don't have the skillset or vision to do what it takes to cars in this kind of condition. So, more often than not, if a car hasn't sold in a short while, it joins the end of the HR queue and turns into a full build.

HR handles everything from start to finish in-house, from rust repair to paintwork, suspension fabrication to build-up and finishing. As someone who's time-served building patina cars, even I find astonishing the speed at which HR builds cars to such a high standard. Youth, energy and passion combined all make the HR business model work – long may it continue.

It takes a lot more effort to carry out sympathetic patina blending on metallic paint, but the HR guys knocked it out of the park on this Strato Silver Oval Bug. (Courtesy Jake Hilling/HR Autoworks)

Jake built this beautiful L87 Pearl White '65 Bug with factory steel sunroof for his girlfriend, Kirby Jarvis. Despite the shine, it is original paint with a great Resto-Cal vibe. (Author's collection)

Cabrio builds are less common, due to the rarity and extra expense of finding rare parts and rebuilding the hood and windows. This one is nearing completion at HR HQ. (Courtesy Jake Hilling/HR Autoworks)

The inside of this Oval window body shows the standard of HR builds. Not many people go this far with patina cars, but this is the HR special sauce. (Courtesy Jake Hilling/HR Autoworks)

What could be better than award-winning street food served out of a Patina Split Single Cab at a VW show? (Courtesy Fresh Rootz)

The Food Vendor
Martin 'Spud' Phazey – Fresh Rootz

I first ran into Fresh Rootz at the 2018 Stonor Park VW show in the UK. Before I'd even realised it was a food truck, I was intrigued by the front of Spud's amazing Patina Single Cab from across the field, and decided to take a closer look. Although I'm not a vegan, the Fresh Rootz menu was tempting, and a cool, refreshing change from the usual junk food offerings at shows. The food was out of this world, and made even better by the cool Patina truck it's served from.

Spud had owned the '59 Single Cab for a few years before deciding it would make a good food truck, upgrading from a Bay Window Westfalia and purpose-built trailer. Far from just a passing fad, Fresh Rootz was a winner of the British Street Food Awards and BBC Good Food Show, and has also appeared on Channel 4's *Sunday Brunch* TV programme.

The Salvager
Drew Pritchard

Star of Discovery Channel's *Salvage Hunters*, Drew Pritchard got into VWs in 1986 at age 17. By this time, he not only knew that he wanted to spend his life buying and selling antiques, but had also begun his training: "From the very first day of the antiques course I was taught about 'minimum intervention'; to preserve the originality of vintage artefacts at all costs.

Drew Pritchard's 1952 Ragtop Beetle pictured outside his antiques shop in Conwy, North Wales. (Author's collection)

Great care was taken to restore Drew's car underneath, without touching the Patina; most of the body and trim has never been apart. (Author's collection)

It's impossible to tell that the bonnet of this car has been sympathetically Patina matched to the rest of the car. (Author's collection)

I've carried the same ethos into everything I've salvaged since. If customers want restored things, then they aren't going to find them in my shop. We preserve things as best as possible, whilst doing the absolute minimum to them in order to keep the original Patina."

Just to prove Drew has been driving Patina VWs longer than most, his first business was started in 1986 with that first rough and ready '67 Beetle; Drew added a roof rack and removed the passenger seat, making it ideally placed to haul home some of his larger finds. Of course, like many of us back in the day, Drew used to drive Patina cars mainly because of a lack of money to buy anything nice, but his love of cars and characterful VWs stuck; at one time he had 14 Beetles, all in various states of repair and decay.

Purchased from the family of the deceased original owner, Drew's 1952 Beetle was sourced new from Germany through an Irish farmer, who was importing cars from Germany before VW Motors (UK) was set up in 1953. When the original owner returned home to the UK, he brought the car with him. In the early years, the car was always garaged until a house move was made in 1976, and the car was hemmed into the garage by all the other Beetles he had by now amassed. Officially there were nine Bugs in total,

Original paint 16in Split Beetle wheels for the car were sourced from across the globe, and are fitted with VW Kübelwagen tyres. (Author's collection)

Drew stands proudly with the car he intends to hold on to forever; many consider an original paint Split Beetle to be the pinnacle of Beetle ownership. (Author's collection)

parked in a line in the driveway; his wife had told him that she would divorce him if his collection got into double figures and it wasn't until after his death that his children found a hidden rental contract for a lock up garage elsewhere with a tenth Beetle inside!

While the car definitely didn't come cheap to Drew, it did come with almost half of its value in New Old Stock parts and panels – having been stored inside for decades, the Bug had survived incredibly well. Despite it only needing front bulkhead repairs, and heater channel bottom plates and outers, which were skilfully repaired, Drew elected to have the car built right; the body was taken off and a full preservation-type restoration was carried out. The floorpan and underside of the car were fully restored, with a few added tweaks to make the car more driveable on modern roads.

The car was fitted with later 15in wheels when purchased, so Drew worked hard to source original 16in Beetle wheels from around the globe; these are shod with 525-16 mud and snow tyres meant for a VW Kübelwagen and give the car a unique look. The wheels are mounted to refurbished rear drum brakes and a neatly hidden disc brake conversion up front. Drew has, however, sourced a set of original finned Porsche 356 brakes and plans to fit these, along with an original set of dull magnesium BRM wheels.

There are no plans to lower the car, so with the BRM wheels fitted, it will look like a pre-Cal Look gasser; a Survivor from the early days of the VW

performance industry. The current engine in the car is a bit of an unknown quantity; while it utilises a 30-horse case, it is thought to be a big bore 1300 with an Okrasa twin carb setup and goes very well, although a larger displacement period performance engine is currently being put together by Ian Clarke of Wolfsburg Performance Services.

When it comes to the bodywork on Drew's car, most of it has never been apart; the only parts that were missing were the front bumper and original bonnet. As an original '52 bonnet couldn't be found, one from a 1953 car was fitted and expertly Patina blended to match the original paint on the rest of the car. Although you literally can't tell the bonnet isn't original, even when standing next to the car, Drew regrets having it matched; like antiques, Drew likes his things to reveal their originality. One thing's for sure when it comes to the '52, it will never be for sale, whatever the future holds for Drew and the antiques industry.

The Picker
Mike Wolfe

Internationally known as the owner of Antique Archaeology and star of History Channel's *American Pickers*, Mike Wolfe is passionate about 'Rusty Gold,' be it antiques and collectables, vintage motorcycles, or classic cars. Mike is openly crazy about vintage Volkswagens and can often be seen on the show driving a Split Single Cab, as well as picking through

Mike Wolfe's enthusiasm for both VWs and 'Rusty Gold' is well publicised on his *American Pickers* show on the History Channel. When Mike gets time at home, outside of his busy schedule, he has this Patina Panel Bus, amongst other VWs and old motorcycles, to play with. (Courtesy Mike Wolfe)

the odd VW junkyard. Mike started out picking in his youth, buying old bicycles out of barns and selling them to antique dealers. When the dealers found out where he was buying them, they asked him to look for other items too.

Although Mike is only seen driving his white Single Cab on American Pickers, he also has an original paint Split Panel Bus with great Patina, and a Split Beetle, which join his huge vintage motorcycle collection. Mike has a particular passion for Indian motorcycles and classic British bikes; whatever you'll find in his collection, you can be sure it has some genuine Patina and 'Rusty Gold.'

The Comedian
Jerry Seinfeld

A longtime classic VW and Porsche enthusiast, Jerry Seinfeld has brought his passion to the screen more recently with his TV series *Comedians in Cars Getting Coffee*, in which he takes fellow comedians out for a drive in cool old cars. For Patina VW enthusiasts, the episode in which Jerry picks up Michael Richards in a Patina 1962 Double Cab Pickup is a must watch.

Jerry Seinfeld stands proudly with his original paint '58 Porsche Speedster, a car that some Porsche 'experts' slated him for spending so much on; Jerry rightfully defended buying the car, on the grounds that there are plenty of restored cars around, but an all-original car is impossible to recreate. (Courtesy Jerry Seinfeld)

When Jerry came out as the highest bidder on an original paint 1958 Porsche 356 Speedster (a hammer price of $583,000 in 2016), he received criticism from *Sports Car Market* magazine (USA) for owning such an expensive Patina car. Jerry's response to the car being called 'abused' and 'neglected?'

"Where is it abused, by the way? What is the abuse? Because someone drove it? Because someone used it to get where they were going? Is that abuse? This was not an art object. That's exactly the charm of it. This is a coveted, thoroughbred sports car that lived its life as just a car to get around. I love that.

"I can't find you another '58 Speedster that has been this used and sat outside and just been a car for all these years and is still in great shape. I couldn't do it with an unlimited budget. But I can find you beautiful, perfect, restored '58 Speedsters all day long.

"I don't know why people have trouble appreciating or perceiving that originality is the end point of what we do. It's got 99k miles on it, seems to have been barely washed in its 57 years, and still runs like a champion – easily keeping up with modern traffic. That, to me, is a fun old car. There is 'original' and then there's Original. This is Original."

The TV Presenter
Jonny Smith

I first learned of Jonny Smith when he worked as a writer, then editor, for *Flat 4/Total VW* magazine, back in the 1990s. Having worked his way up the car magazine ranks, he was then invited to do a

The car that started it all for Jonny Smith; the original Zenith Blue '67 1500 Beetle that he used to write about in *Flat 4/Total VW* magazines while he worked for Jazz Publishing, and which he bought at the tender age of 16. (Courtesy Jonny Smith)

Actor, philanthropist, and gearhead Ewan McGregor manages to combine two of his passions in one with his original paint VW Single Cab; the truck is a useful workhorse, meaning he can transport his vintage Moto Guzzi motorcycles in the back, as well as using the truck to do more mundane things like picking up his Christmas tree, as he was doing when photographed here. (Courtesy Splash)

screen test for Channel 5's *Fifth Gear* programme, which he presents alongside Tiff Needell and Vicky Butler-Henderson. This led to his own program, *Industrial Junkie*, and a new BBC America series, *Mud, Sweat & Gears*.

Despite owning a diverse collection of cars, from a ratty '68 Dodge Charger, to a '64 Chevy Impala SS, to his 'Flux Capacitor' – a classic British Enfield electric car converted to modern EV power and used for drag racing – Jonny still owns the '67 Zenith Blue Beetle he bought when he was just 16. While the car, which sports a large amount of original paint and Patina, has been off the road for some years, it will see the light of day again in the future – as soon as Jonny has all the parts he needs to put it back on the road.

The Movie Star
Ewan McGregor

Shooting to fame in the film *Trainspotting* in 1996, Ewan has gone on to star in the Star Wars films, become an ambassador for UNICEF, and take crazy motorcycle adventures Long Way Round and Long Way Down with sidekick Charley Boorman. Ewan had a VW Beetle as his first car in Scotland, and his passion grew from there. Although he now calls Los Angeles home, VWs are still his hobby, owning a restored Jeans Beetle on air ride, a beautiful stock Oval Window Bug, and an amazing original paint Single Cab, amongst others. Whilst Ewan is a private person, he can occasionally be seen at Californian VW events, where he will happily chat to fellow VW enthusiasts and have his picture taken with them.

CHAPTER SIX

Origins & ownership

The cars & their stories

From the moment the idea for this book came to me, I knew there were thousands of Volkswagens with amazing Patina that could be featured in it. As I came to put the pictures together though, I realised that this book is as much about the owners as it is the cars themselves; not just the current owner, but all the previous owners who

have added history to the incredible cars within this book.

Having owned a lot of original paint Volkswagens myself, I can attest to the fact that a good story attached to a car always makes it that much more special. Some cars come with a known history; they may be a one owner car that's been stored away

Gerson Ampessan's '72 Brazilian Beetle was the subject of a full body-off restoration underneath, but the Patina was kept on the body. The Brazilian cars look very different to European production cars, as they had early pre-'65 thick window pillars, but updated bumpers and other parts. (Courtesy Gerson Douglas Ampessan)

for decades, or a car with several owners but full documentation – what the classic car industry defines as provenance – but even if there's just one cool story devoted to the car, that one story makes the car a part of VW folklore, and thus adds a further degree of uniqueness.

Continues on page 144

You wouldn't believe how rough Mike Heywood's Garnet Red '58 Beetle looked when he first got it. The finished build shows how good his skills are at bringing these cars back to life. Having always built lowered cars, Mike decided to build this one stock height on Crossply tyres for a more original look. (Author's collection)

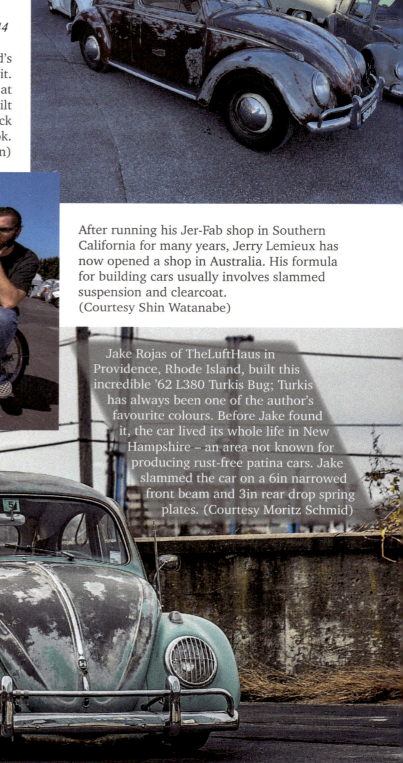

After running his Jer-Fab shop in Southern California for many years, Jerry Lemieux has now opened a shop in Australia. His formula for building cars usually involves slammed suspension and clearcoat. (Courtesy Shin Watanabe)

Jake Rojas of TheLuftHaus in Providence, Rhode Island, built this incredible '62 L380 Turkis Bug; Turkis has always been one of the author's favourite colours. Before Jake found it, the car lived its whole life in New Hampshire – an area not known for producing rust-free patina cars. Jake slammed the car on a 6in narrowed front beam and 3in rear drop spring plates. (Courtesy Moritz Schmid)

Jerry Lemieux's old 'Burnt Westy' was once next to a house that caught fire, giving it a unique Patina after being stored outside for decades. (Courtesy Shin Watanabe)

Joel Herman decided to deviate from the usual look by fitting wide 16in Fuchs wheels to the back of his slammed Gulf Blue Ragtop. (Courtesy Joel Herman)

Jeff Marton has amassed a cool collection of Patina Volkswagens, including a logoed Single Cab with very little of the original Sealing Wax Red paint left on it. (Courtesy Jeff Marton)

Sam Trigg nailed it with the stance on his '57 Oval Beetle, seen here at the 2017 DTA meet. The car features a fully restored underside and interior. (Courtesy Joss Ashley)

It's rare to see Fastbacks get the recognition they deserve, especially when compared with other Type 3 models. Jason Jongeneelen from Riverside, California did this one justice with clearcoat and a full interior and underside resto. (Courtesy Jason Jongeneelen)

Dave Hall's old Barndoor Bus was fitted with wind-up side windows by a coachbuilder in the 1950s. The metal restoration was done while the Bus was in Matt Smith's ownership, but it was Dave who lowered it and stripped it back to the original factory primer. (Author's collection)

Darren Franklin has a thing about Patina logo buses and, at the last count, he owned four; there's something about Patina and original logos that gets hardcore Bus guys going. (Courtesy Darren Franklin)

It's very hard to recreate beautiful time-worn Patina like that on Jeff Marton's Single Cab. (Courtesy Jeff Marton)

The California-based half of the French Vintage Autohaus VW import business, Fabien Becasse, sources cars and has built a few of his own VWs, including this cool logoed pressed bumper Panel Bus. (Courtesy Fabien Becasse)

I realised this while researching Chapter Five; I spent an evening on the phone to four different VW guys in the USA, and really fed off their enthusiasm and excitement, especially when it came to telling the stories of their cars. Brendan Finn, for example, became incredibly animated when talking about his most recent find: a '59 Double Cab discovered in Montana, which was sold new at Evel Knievel's grandfather's Volkswagen dealership – Knievel Imports in Butte, Montana.

The added excitement that this one historical fact brought to Brendan (and myself – we both had Evel Knievel toy motorcycles during the late '70s) was clear in his voice, and reverberated through the phone, even though an ocean separated us. Similar was the enthusiasm of Gibbs Connors when talking about discovering the King Panel Bus

After spending a few years driving around his California home in a fully restored and lowered 13-window Split Bus, Rolando Alvarado sold it, and built this awesome Patina Panel Bus. (Courtesy Derek 'Boxrod' Campbell)

The VW-based Puma GT was originally called the Malzoni GT, after company founder Genaro Malzoni, and was designed to compete in the highly competitive Brazilian GT Racing Series. It was the first plant production Brazilian sportscar, as well as being manufactured in kit form. Lewis Heywood's '77 Puma now calls the UK home and sits a lot closer to the floor, courtesy of the air-ride installed by Max and Jesse at Eva Resto. Wheels are original MAG Industries. (Courtesy Lewis Heywood)

It sparked a debate on social media when Justin Marino decided to paint blend the upper half of his Bus in Palm Green, to replace the paint burned-off by the sun. Whatever side of the debate you're on though, there's no denying that the Bus has a great look. (Courtesy Derek 'Boxrod' Campbell)

on his doorstep, only two miles from the Volkswagen dealership that sold it new. Like me, I'm sure you understand why Gibbs called the phone number logoed on the side of the original paint Bus, and can appreciate his excitement when the original owner's sister picked up the phone.

I have a similar story of my own, from 1998; I'd bought a 1971 VW Danbury Camper in the UK, which had lots of old documentation, including the original owner's name and address. A long shot, I wrote a letter to the original owner in all likelihood that the guy didn't still live there. I was blown away when he replied, including the original Volkswagen purchase invoice and the original Danbury Motorcaravans brochure he'd got from the VW dealer in 1971.

Continues on page 148

Karl Fennell's 1960 Mango Green/Seagull Grey Bus received the best of everything during the build. As well as the beautifully polished original paint and suspension modifications, it had a bespoke Oak camping interior built, and all the details were very high-end. (Courtesy Karl Fennell)

Dave Hall's incredible Barndoor 23-window Bus was discovered in a Swedish forest; it had rusted so badly that it was shipped back to the UK in pieces. Matt Smith at Smiths VW in Cornwall, UK did an amazing job of piecing it back together. (Courtesy Joss Ashley)

One of the most anticipated VW builds on Instagram of 2017, Mike Heywood's '63 Bug features the burned-off remains of an old dark green repaint, with the original L380 Turkis showing through. (Courtesy Joss Ashley)

The Deutsche Bundespost had its own VW colour, but not many knew that other customers could special order this colour too. Tiffany McDonald's 1960 Single Cab was shipped out to California when new, and has spent its life getting wonderfully sunburned. (Courtesy 10_FT Doug)

Whatever your opinion on clearcoated Patina, there's no denying it gives cars a unique look, as with Diego Vazquez' hardcore Patina Bug. (Courtesy Bait Media)

PJ Gibbons' '51 Beetle was given a full body-off restoration after sitting since 1975, first in a Swedish barn, then outside under a tarpaulin. The car runs on original magnesium Porsche 'Gas Burner' wheels and has a Porsche 356/Okrasa engine. (Courtesy PJ Gibbons)

The DTA 2017 Show, based in the old James Cond Printworks in Birmingham, UK, showcased the best Patina cars the country has to offer. (Courtesy Joss Ashley)

On the flip side, I've bought a lot of cars which didn't come with any history at all; I often looked at these cars and wondered what their story was, and felt sad that I had no clue what had happened to the car over the last 40 or 50 years. This makes you really grasp at small details that might lead you to discover more about the car, maybe grinning from ear to ear when one day you discover an old photo online and realise that it's an old photo of YOUR car.

I once bought an original paint Mouse Grey 1963 Walkthru Bus that came out of a junkyard called A1 Auto Salvage in Roswell, New Mexico. I don't think there's a person in the Western world that doesn't know the Roswell alien stories, so this alone added some folklore to my newest purchase.

Finding an old picture of my Bus online, sitting in the junkyard, with a '65 Bug sitting on its roof, also gave me some insight into the life that it had lived in the junkyard, and why I now needed to spend so much time straightening the roof! Discovering the original New Mexico licence plate, kindly sent to me by Matt Weatherly – the guy who discovered the Bus and liberated it from the junkyard – put the final piece of the jigsaw in place; the

licence plate had a 1973 tag on it, proving that the Bus had been sitting since it was ten years old.

The best bit about having the licence plate in my hands was the history it revealed. During its 40 years in the junkyard, the hot sun had baked off almost all of the yellow and red paint, yet the original Mouse Grey and Pearl White paint had fared much better. Knowing that the Bus had only spent ten years of its life on the road also solved the mystery of why the brake linings were all original, and the king and link pins were in such good shape; I'd never seen original

A longtime member of the German Folks Klub (GFK), Rich Rivera usually builds show quality cars, but this original paint '58 Ragtop Bug was too nice to restore. (Courtesy Richard Rivera)

Patina isn't just about the exterior paint on a vehicle, as shown by the perfectly Patinated horn button on Billy Davila's Deluxe Microbus. (Courtesy Billy Davila)

When Paul Pace bought Seaside Neil's Oval Bug, he had a very different vision of how the car should look; it's amazing the difference a new stance and wheels can make to a car. (Courtesy Dave Hall)

VW brake linings in 27 years of VW ownership, despite owning around 100 classic Volkswagens.

The origin of any car can be discovered if you're prepared to do some digging; they may not come with a full log of the ownership history, original documentation, or large folder of old receipts, but finding one great old picture or even some small items when cleaning out the inside of a new purchase, are all precious clues.

The great thing about Patina cars, of course, is that the paint itself adds provenance; it tells an honest story of 40, 50, or 60 years of use (the way a restored car never can); it tells of hot summers and harsh winters outside, or of a more cosseted existence inside a dry garage, safe from the ice and snow, or shaded from the searing sun.

The author first saw the now-legendary 1968 Tinoc tonic water-logoed Bay Window Panel Van at Le Bug Show in Spa, Belgium in 2006, but didn't have the money to become the new owner. It was bought by Paul Machin of The Bus Barn and brought to the UK, where it was slammed on original South African Sprintstar/Rostyle wheels. It later belonged to a succession of owners, the last of whom left it outside for many years. When Darren Adams finally managed to buy it, it was in a sorry state. Darren sympathetically restored it, with the help of VW Aircooled Works in Spalding. (Courtesy Joss Ashley/Hayburner and author's collection)

Many of us have a car we have sold and look back on fondly, some of us have many. We all have stories of 'the one that got away,' that we regret selling, especially now that prices have risen and we may never be able to afford to buy it back, if they're even for sale.

Some may be lucky enough to re-own a past love and vow never to let it slip away again, where others may get to own a car that they've coveted for the second time, yet decide to let it go again. Sentimentality is a funny thing and so is scarcity; it's human nature for things that we can't have to appear more attractive, and when we have them, sometimes the novelty disappears once they are seemingly no longer scarce.

Whatever happens though, the fact that you've owned a car has added to its history. Maybe you've carried out some preservation or restoration work,

taken extended road trips in it and added a few extra miles to the odometer, have some funny breakdown stories or memories of when you fixed a car by the side of the road and completed your trip. All of this, whether you now own the car or not, is a valuable addition to the car's past, especially if you told the story on an internet forum, through social media, or shared the story with the car's next owner.

I guess this is why I, and many others, have such a problem with 'Fake Rat Look' type cars, where the paint has been forcefully sanded off and intentionally allowed to rust. When this car changes hands in the future – and it will – the timestamp added, by fake rusting it and causing it to deteriorate at a faster rate than nature intended, will be one that actually serves to shorten the life of the car, not enhance nature's Patina.

When it comes to owning Patina Volkswagens, I'm a firm believer that we're only temporary custodians of these cars and we should be doing our best to not only preserve them for future generations to enjoy but also to educate others along these lines.

If you're into Fake Rat Look cars, and disappointed by the lack of pictures of them in this book (except to illustrate the look), then I can explain; fake rust isn't, and never will be, true Patina. There's a huge difference in sympathetically matching a body panel on a car that Mother Nature has Patinated herself, such as

It takes a lot of years of sun exposure to create genuine Patina like this on Robert Ramsey's bullet-nose Dove Blue Kombi.
(Courtesy Robert Ramsey)

Double Cab Pickups have rated high up on the Bus lover's desirability scale for many years; Robert Ramsey's truck is a true Patina Survivor.
(Courtesy Robert Ramsey)

the missing rear wing on Jeff Laughlin's Beryl Green '63 Bug, or the bonnet on Drew Pritchard's '52; both of which respectfully finish off an already beautiful Patina car, by carefully matching paint and the original Patina markings.

Hopefully, if you've committed the Fake Rat crime on a car at some point, having read this far, you might now realise the error of your ways; remember that you're just the custodian of each car you own and it deserves to live a long and dignified life after your ownership.

Chip Rodriguez is just one of the guys who 'gets it'; his incredible original paint Anthracite Notchback is just as well preserved now as when he bought it in 2001. I first saw the car at the Bug-In 33 show in California in 2008, and took a couple of pictures of it; at the time, I was blown away by the amazing original condition of the car and the lovely light Patina fade on a few areas. It was years later that I realised that Chip was the owner and connected with

him through Instagram; the car became even more special in my mind when I discovered the story behind not only how he came to own it, but also how many years he'd had it.

Chip bought the car in 1991 from the original

Originally built by Johnny Danger in Germany, this January '51 Bus is a Patina monster. (Courtesy Mike Johnson)

Japan has a reputation for turning out amazing Patina cars, such as Masayuki Miura's awesome L380 Turkis Bug on Fuchs wheels. Cars like this can't help but tell an interesting story. (Courtesy Niels Timmerman)

Having owned the car since 1991, the year he bought it from the original owner, Chip Rodriguez's Anthracite Grey '63 Notchback is as 'Survivor' as it gets. (Courtesy 10_ft Doug)

owners, Bert and Mary Wichmann, who bought the car new from Aeroway Motors in Brampton, Ontario, Canada on June 20, 1963. He vowed to keep the car all original and to never sell it. Chip has kept his promise for 27 years so far, and shared with me a heartwarming story about dropping in on the original owners in 2009; they were delighted and emotional to see 'Charlie' was in the same condition they'd sold it in all those years ago. Bert shook Chip's hand and warmly thanked him for keeping his word.

The reason I'm telling Chip's story, despite the fact it's a great one, is to illustrate what VW ownership means to different people. Most of us in the VW scene change cars pretty often (some with alarming regularity), they are 'stepping stone' cars, as Brendan Finn puts it; the cars that are bought and sold to 'trade up' to their dream or forever car. Others may never own a car they want to keep; for these guys the joy they get from old VWs is picking them up, restoring or preserving them in some way, then passing them along for someone else to enjoy, before being tempted by yet another car they just 'have to own.' For some, it's enough to be able to say they owned something special, even if for a short time.

Randy Carlson also has a great story to tell as the proud owner of 'Randy's VW'; a Beetle that was formerly owned and treasured by well-respected junkyard owner Randy Pollack: "... Randy's VW

Martin Feast has owned his L50H Brilliant Blue 1970 Deluxe Bay Window Bus for 17+ years; the Bus is lowered courtesy of a link pin front beam and drop spindles. Martin bought the Bus for $600 out of a Missouri junkyard. (Author's collection)

Mango Green was a one year only colour for Bugs, and is quite rare to see; Martin Feast's slammed 1960 RHD original paint car features air ride and Rostyle wheels. (Author's collection)

Austin Working picked an unusual base on which to build his hardcore Patina car: a 1968 Beetle. Whatever your beliefs on late-model VWs, no-one can deny that Austin's car is Patina perfection and tells a long and interesting story. (Courtesy Austin Working)

Many consider a US spec 1967 Beetle to be the ultimate basis for a traditional or Old School Cal Look car; Bertrand Tomazic from France has given this Patina '67 the look with some original EMPI parts. (Courtesy Bertrand Tomazic)

Jason Reich is a guy who likes to find the very best survivor cars available on which to base his projects. He then builds them so that everything bar the paint on the body is new, so they can start a new life. His Highwheeler project is very unusual (especially in the USA) as he chose a late model 'Fat Chick' car and chose to go high rather than low with this build. The wheels are from Mobelwagen, which Jason stocks at his company Aircooled Vintage Works. (Courtesy Jason Reich/Aircooled Vintage Works)

Rikki James has owned his original paint RHD 1954 Barndoor Deluxe for many years, after it was imported from Sweden in the late 1990s. Rikki has been an active, long-time member of the UK Split Screen Van Club (SSVC), and can be seen at many UK VW events in his bus. Rikki is another guy who had a Patina Bus before Patina was even a thing; his Bus has a 2.6-litre Type 4 engine and can often be seen terrorising modern cars on the highway. (Courtesy Rikki James)

can remain Randy's VW ... but with a different Randy," Carlson told me. The car is a 1960 stock, through and through, and rusted in several spots too. "... It is spectacularly bad, but is an amazing artefact and representation of what Mother Nature can accomplish with a car in a certain climate. I drive it often and proudly."

Like Brendan Finn, and others I've had the good fortune to interview for this book, Drew Pritchard also favours a phrase which I hope will stick when it comes to preserving Patina Volkswagens: "minimum intervention." It means doing the minimum amount to a car in order to make it roadworthy, and preserve it for future generations to enjoy.

In these days of social media transience, when pictures come and go or are lost forever when forums inevitably crash or shut down, I like to think that this book captures the history of Patina VWs to date. Print media may well be giving way to digital, but you can't beat having a physical book in your hands, that you can keep on a dusty bookshelf, and refer to for decades to come.

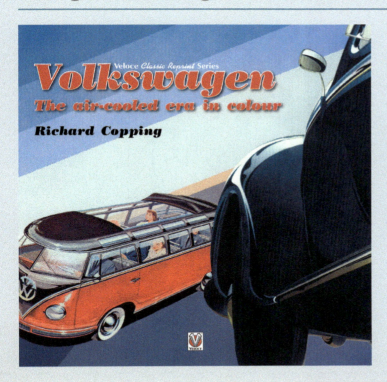
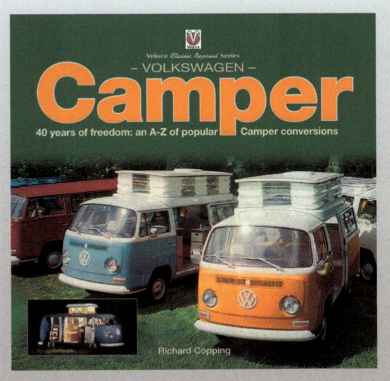

More great Volkswagen books from Veloce ...

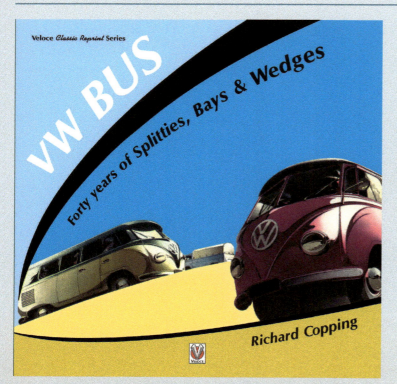
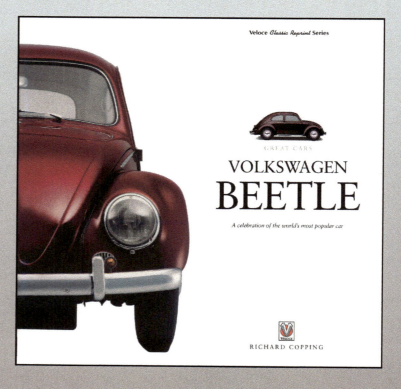

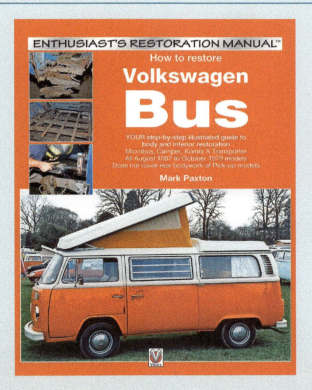

A complete guide to the restoration of your VW Bus, with full coverage of body and chassis repairs, suspension, steering and brakes, plus trim and paint. It also covers the tools, equipment and workshop techniques needed to make your Bus look like new once more.

ISBN: 978-1-845840-93-8
Paperback • 27x20.7cm • 272 pages
• 1110 colour and b&w pictures

Available again!
Written by an enthusiast the How to Restore Volkswagen Beetle Enthusiasts Restoration Manual is the only up-to-date book dealing with a complete Beetle restoration – from basic skills required, to dealing with professional restorers. The perfect book, whether you have no technical knowledge, or are an old hand at restoring!

ISBN: 978-1-845849-46-7
Paperback • 27x20.7cm • 224 pages
• c.700 colour pictures

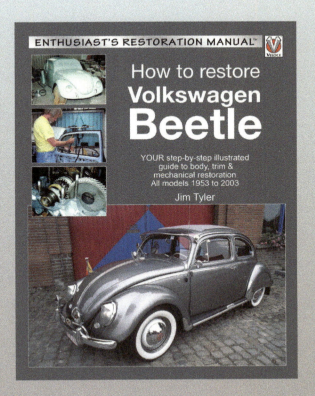

More great Volkswagen books from Veloce ...

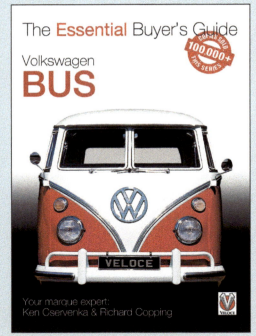

ISBN: 978-1-845840-22-8

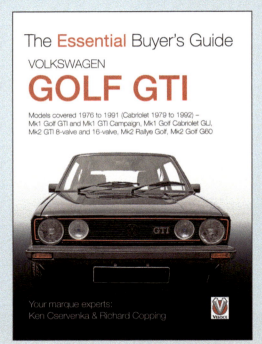

ISBN: 978-1-845841-88-1

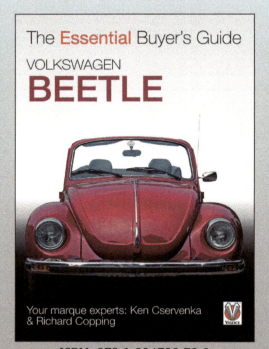

ISBN: 978-1-904788-72-0

Having these books in your pocket is just like having a real marque expert by your side. Benefit from the author's years of real ownership experience, learn how to spot a bad vehicle quickly, and how to assess a promising one like a professional. Get the right car at the right price!

Paperback • 19.5x13.9cm • 64 pages

For more information and price details, visit our website at www.veloce.co.uk
email: info@veloce.co.uk • Tel: +44(0)1305 260068

Index